The Complete Guide to

GROWING VEGETABLES, FLOWERS, FRUITS, AND HERBS FROM CONTAINERS

Everything You
Need To Know
Explained Simply

By Lizz Shepherd

THE COMPLETE GUIDE TO GROWING VEGETABLES, FLOWERS, FRUITS, AND HERBS FROM CONTAINERS: EVERYTHING YOU NEED TO KNOW EXPLAINED SIMPLY

Library of Congress Cataloging-in-Publication Data

Shepherd, Lizz, 1974-
  The complete guide to growing vegetables, flowers, fruits, and herbs from containers : everything you need to know explained simply / by: Lizz Shepherd.
     p. cm.
  Includes bibliographical references and index.
  ISBN-13: 978-1-60138-347-1 (alk. paper)
  ISBN-10: 1-60138-347-9 (alk. paper)
  1. Container gardening. I. Title.
  SB418.S54 2011
  635.9'86--dc22
                         2010044150

Printed in the United States

PROJECT MANAGER: Melissa Peterson
PROOFING • Gretchen Pressley • phygem@gmail.com
INTERIOR LAYOUT: Antoinette D'Amore • addesign@videotron.ca
COVER DESIGN: Meg Buchner • meg@megbuchner.com
BACK COVER DESIGN: Jackie Miller • millerjackiej@gmail.com

Printed on Recycled Paper

We recently lost our beloved pet "Bear," who was not only our best and dearest friend but also the "Vice President of Sunshine" here at Atlantic Publishing. He did not receive a salary but worked tirelessly 24 hours a day to please his parents. Bear was a rescue dog that turned around and showered myself, my wife, Sherri, his grandparents Jean, Bob, and Nancy, and every person and animal he met (maybe not rabbits) with friendship and love. He made a lot of people smile every day.

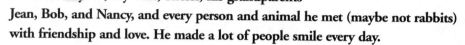

We wanted you to know that a portion of the profits of this book will be donated to The Humane Society of the United States. *–Douglas & Sherri Brown*

The human-animal bond is as old as human history. We cherish our animal companions for their unconditional affection and acceptance. We feel a thrill when we glimpse wild creatures in their natural habitat or in our own backyard.

Unfortunately, the human-animal bond has at times been weakened. Humans have exploited some animal species to the point of extinction.

The Humane Society of the United States makes a difference in the lives of animals here at home and worldwide. The HSUS is dedicated to creating a world where our relationship with animals is guided by compassion. We seek a truly humane society in which animals are respected for their intrinsic value, and where the human-animal bond is strong.

Want to help animals? We have plenty of suggestions. Adopt a pet from a local shelter, join The Humane Society and be a part of our work to help companion animals and wildlife. You will be funding our educational, legislative, investigative and outreach projects in the U.S. and across the globe.

Or perhaps you'd like to make a memorial donation in honor of a pet, friend or relative? You can through our Kindred Spirits program. And if you'd like to contribute in a more structured way, our Planned Giving Office has suggestions about estate planning, annuities, and even gifts of stock that avoid capital gains taxes.

Maybe you have land that you would like to preserve as a lasting habitat for wildlife. Our Wildlife Land Trust can help you. Perhaps the land you want to share is a backyard—that's enough. Our Urban Wildlife Sanctuary Program will show you how to create a habitat for your wild neighbors.

So you see, it's easy to help animals. And The HSUS is here to help.

2100 L Street NW • Washington, DC 20037 • 202-452-1100
www.hsus.org

Trademark Disclaimer

Dedication

To my beautiful grandmothers,
Nellie Fullerton and the late Helen Fowler,
and to my children, Arianna, Miranda, and Leo.

Table of Contents

Introduction **15**

What Container Gardening Can — and Cannot — do for You 16

Plants that Thrive in Containers 17

How to Use This Book 17

Chapter 1: Why Garden in Containers? **19**

How Plants Grow Naturally 20

    Why container gardening works 20

Space Constraints 21

Easy Portability 21

    Ideal for renters or temporary residents 22

    Ideal for growing food between seasons 22

Inhospitable Terrain 22

    Too much or not enough sun 23

    Too hot or too cold 24

    Too much or not enough rain 25

    Apartment or condo dwellers might not have
    any "ground" to plant in 26

Aesthetic Appeal 27

    Easily change the look of the yard or accommodate different events 27

Decorate specific areas that might not be equipped to sustain in-ground plants *28*

For Food 29

Save money at the grocery store *29*

Always have a ready supply of fresh, nutrient-dense produce *30*

Know where your food is coming from and what has been used to produce it *30*

Case Study: Growing Indoors versus Outdoors 32

Chapter 2: What Should I Grow? **35**

Grow Plants that are Well-Adapted to Your Environmental Conditions and Weather 35

Grow Plants that Suit Your USDA Hardiness Zone 36

Grow Plants You Enjoy Eating 37

Grow foods you already like and new variations of old favorites *38*

Grow Plants that Work Well in Containers 40

What type of plant works well in containers? *40*

What type of plant does not grow well in containers? *41*

Grow Plants that Complement Your Garden or Décor 42

Planting a large container with multiple plants *43*

Grow Plants You Can Maintain 44

Know your time constraints *45*

Which plants require little maintenance? *45*

Which plants require a lot of maintenance? *49*

Case Study: Why Grow in Containers? 52

Chapter 3: Choosing and Preparing Containers for Growing **55**

Size Matters 55

Container Composition 57

Plastic *57*

Clay *58*

Concrete...*58*

Wood..*59*

Paper..*59*

Glass..*60*

Recycled and "art" planters *61*

Container Types...61

Hanging..*62*

Window box..*62*

Garden pots..*63*

Oversized planters...*63*

Containers Come in all Sizes and Shapes 64

The Importance of Drainage..65

Water is good for plants, right?...*66*

Chapter 4: Tools **69**

Gloves...69

Trowel 71

Shovel..72

Clippers/Pruning Shears 73

Watering Can 73

Cultivating Fork 75

String or Garden Ties..75

Stakes or Trellises 76

Case Study: A Love for Gardening..78

Chapter 5: Soil and Amendments **81**

Choosing the Right Soil 82

Using a Quality Soil Blend 83

Fertilizers...*84*

Watering granules...*86*

Case Study: From the Perspective of a New Container Garden 87

Chapter 6: Start with Seeds or Start with Plants? 89

Why Start with Seeds? 90

Why Start with Plants? 90

Seeds 91

Buying seeds 91

Heirloom seeds 91

Hybrid seeds 92

How seeds work 93

How to plant seeds 93

Starting seeds indoors 94

Transplanting your seedlings 95

Plants 95

Choosing plants 95

Buying plants 97

Re-potting your purchased plants 97

Companion Planting 98

Case Study: Straight from the Expert 99

Chapter 7: Growing Herbs in Containers 101

Food Use 101

Medicinal Use 102

Bath and Beauty Use 102

Home Cleaning and Décor Use 103

Herbs are Easy to Grow in Containers 103

A Complete List of Container-grown Herbs 104

Basil 105

Borage 106

Chamomile 108

Chives 110

Cilantro..*112*

Dill...*113*

Fennel..*115*

Lavender..*117*

Mint...*119*

Oregano...*121*

Parsley...*123*

Rosemary..*126*

Sage...*129*

Thyme..*131*

Great Herb Garden Combinations...133

Italian cooking garden...*134*

Kitchen garden...*135*

Medicinal garden..*136*

Common Mistakes to Avoid when Growing Herbs.....................139

Case Study: Straight from the Expert.......................................143

Chapter 8: Growing Vegetables in Containers......................145

Can You Really Grow Vegetables in Containers? 146

Why Grow Your Own Vegetables? 149

To save money at the grocery store..*150*

To know where your food is coming from..................................*151*

To teach your children about growing and science *152*

To put flavorful, nutritious, fresh food at your fingertips.....................*154*

Vegetables are very easy to grow
and respond well to containers of all types................................*155*

A Complete List of Container-grown Vegetables....................156

Beans...*156*

Carrots...*159*

Cucumbers...*161*

Garlic...*163*

Lettuce and salad greens *165*

Onions *168*

Peas *170*

Potatoes *172*

Spinach *174*

Squash *176*

Zucchini *178*

Common Mistakes to Avoid when Growing Vegetables 180

Case Study: Using Containers in Small Spaces 182

Chapter 9: Growing Fruits in Containers **185**

Can You Really Grow Fruits in Containers? 186

Why Grow Your Own Fruit? 187

Ornamental Fruit *187*

A Complete List of Container-grown Fruits 189

Blueberries *189*

Raspberries *191*

Blackberries *192*

Gooseberries *194*

Citrus fruit *195*

Lemon *196*

Lime *198*

Currants *200*

Grapes *203*

Cantaloupe *206*

Watermelon *207*

Honeydew *209*

Peaches *211*

Strawberries *213*

Tomatoes *216*

Common Mistakes to Avoid when Growing Fruit 218

Case Study: Gardening through the Years 221

Chapter 10: Growing Flowers in Containers 225

Can You Grow Any Type of Flowers in Containers?.............................226

Why Grow Your Own Flowers? 226

A Complete List of Container-grown Flowers...............................227

Roses...............................*227*

Flowers from bulbs...............................*230*

Daffodils...............................*232*

Tulips *233*

Amaryllis *235*

Hyacinth...............................*237*

Gladiolus *240*

Lily...............................*242*

Flowers from seeds *245*

Marigolds...............................*245*

Zinnias...............................*247*

Sunflowers...............................*249*

Growing Perennial Flowers in Containers 252

Edible Flowers 252

Succulents...............................257

Common Mistakes to Avoid when Growing Flowers 259

Case Study: Container Gardening Tips...............................260

Chapter 11: MaintainingYour Plants 261

Pest Management...............................262

Troubleshooting Common Problems 267

Pruning 269

Replanting...............................270

Learning From Others 271

Taking gardening classes *271*

Swapping seeds and seedlings *272*

Finding local help *272*

Conclusion **275**

Anyone Can Garden in Containers 275

Container Gardening is Flexible, Affordable, and Fun 276

Appendix A: USDA Plant Hardiness Zone Map **277**

Bibliography **279**

Author Biography **283**

Index **285**

Introduction

Container gardening is a fun and easy alternative to outdoor gardening for many people who want to grow their own food and flowers. Growing fresh fruits, vegetables, and herbs at home throughout the year is a healthy alternative to surviving on processed food. However, for many people, gardening outdoors throughout the year is not possible, whether due to apartment living, limited yard space, or physical limitations. Thankfully, container gardening offers an alternative to anyone with these limitations.

Quite simply, container gardening is the process of growing plants in containers. Although many container gardens are started indoors because of space or climate limitations, you can also grow plants in containers outdoors by placing the containers in your yard, on your driveway, or on a porch or balcony. Virtually any outdoor area can be accessorized with the right container and a beautiful, thriving plant.

For many people, container gardening is about the very best use of available space. With the use of plant shelves, hanging pots, and other space-saving container arrangements, many types of plants can be grown in a small space. One small balcony can house dozens of plants, produce, and flowers.

Container gardening has been used for centuries. The ancient Romans used container plants to decorate their balconies and rooftops and to provide ready food sources. The ancient Egyptians and Babylonians also used containers to grow plants for food and ornamental flowers and trees.

What Container Gardening Can — and Cannot — do for You

Container gardening can grow a variety of produce and flowers, but there is a limit to the size of the plants that can be grown. Fast-growing trees and large bushes, for example, would be difficult to grow in a container. Those plants generally have root systems that will grow larger than the volume of a typical container. Container gardening is generally used to create small quantities of produce and a few plants of each variety. This type of gardening is not practical if you want to grow large quantities of crops that will become your only food source.

Container gardening can, however, replace much of the produce you normally buy, which will save you time and reduce your grocery bill significantly. It is also an enjoyable hobby; it can be rewarding to see your tiny seedlings grow into large, strong plants. It provides an educational activity for children and a way for couples to engage in a hobby together.

Your first food and/or flower crop is not likely to be your best, as it takes time to understand how to nurture plants and provide the best environment for each type. You can expect subsequent years to provide a more bountiful crop with less trial and error on your part.

Plants that Thrive in Containers

Most plants that do not have sprawling root systems can be grown in a container. Small vegetable plants are popular choices for indoor growing, including carrots, cucumbers, beans, onions, garlic, lettuce, peas, potatoes, spinach, squash, and zucchini.

Fruit may not seem like the typical container crop, but many fruit plants are well suited to being grown in containers. Some fruit trees or bushes take up large amounts of space vertically and horizontally and must be grown in large containers, so the containers might need to be placed outdoors because of space considerations in the home. This is the case for blueberries and other berry bushes. Other fruits that can be grown in containers are tomatoes, currants, grapes, melons, citrus fruits, peaches, and strawberries.

Herbs are perhaps one of the most popular types of indoor edible plants because the plants are generally compact in size. Typical container herbs include basil, borage, chamomile, chives, cilantro, dill, fennel, lavender, mint, oregano, parsley, rosemary, sage, and thyme. Growing even a dozen small herb plants only takes up a small amount of space and can supply enough fresh herbs to cook with every day, year round.

The range of flowers that can be grown in containers is limited only by size. Although some flowers are more likely to thrive when grown indoors than others, most flowering plants can be grown in a container as long as it is cared for properly. Roses, daffodils, tulips, amaryllis, African violets, lilies, marigolds, zinnias, sunflowers, and pansies are just some of the flowers that can be grown in containers, as can most small flowering plants that thrive at room temperature.

How to Use This Book

Although you might be interested in growing just one specific type of plant, this book has information that can help expand the range of plants in which you are interested. You might use this book to reference information specifically about growing tomatoes in a container and find that your gardening skills and supplies will enable you to grow other fruits and vegetables you also love.

Before growing a new plant, reference this book to find the needed supplies and required growing conditions. You can search for the information by simply locating the exact plant you want to grow or by studying the basic plant types, such as herbs or fruits. To find out which plants will grow best in your location, study the United States Department of Agriculture (USDA) Hardiness Zone map, the climate recommendations, and the amount of light they need to survive. All of these factors must be taken into consideration when choosing which plants to grow.

If you are determined to grow a plant indoors, even though its requirements for success do not match the conditions in your home, special equipment, such as ultraviolet (UV) lamps, humidifiers, and dehumidifiers, can be used to recreate the plant's natural environment. Recreating this environment can be a painstaking task that requires ongoing maintenance, but it is possible if you understand the conditions each plant needs to thrive.

As a beginner container gardener, you need to know a good deal of basic information to keep your plants healthy and producing. Once you have finished this book, you will understand all of the variables involved with growing plants in containers and will be able to grow a wide variety of flowers as well as any number of edible items. Instead of running to the store and choosing from the high-priced produce grown by someone else, you can wake up among your own crop and have your choice of produce whenever you need it.

Chapter 1

WHY GARDEN IN CONTAINERS?

There are as many reasons to grow plants in containers as there are gardeners who love to tend these plants. In some cases, a number of factors make outdoor gardening inconvenient or impossible. For some people, bending and stooping to care for plants growing in the ground are physically difficult. Having the option to place containers on a table or shelf can allow those people to do the gardening they enjoy.

Climate reasons also might make it more practical to plant in containers. In desert regions, the intense heat and sunlight make it hard for many people to enjoy outside activities such as gardening. In the southwest United States, a 110-degree day is not unusual, and staying outdoors for hours at a time to tend plants on those days is not only uncomfortable but also sometimes dangerous. Being able to garden inside or on a shaded patio can accommodate gardeners in these conditions.

Soil issues, such as having thick clay soil or soil with a high sand content, can make it difficult to grow certain plants in the ground. Clay in particular is difficult to till and mix with fertilizer and potting soil. Tilling the soil often requires renting heavy equipment to break through the top layer of the clay to begin the process. In those areas, it is far easier and more productive to grow the items in containers and place them on the ground, inside the house, in window boxes, or in any other available space.

How Plants Grow Naturally

Plants generally need only a few things to grow and produce fruit, vegetables, herbs, berries, or flowers: space, air circulation around the plant, the right soil containing specific nutrients, water, and varying amounts of sunlight so chlorophyll within the leaves can create the plant's vital food: starch, which fuels the growth of the plant.

Because many of the plants we grow today did not originate in the areas where we live, it is usually necessary to recreate at least some of the conditions of the plant's native land to keep the plant growing its best. This might be as simple as watering the plant regularly, but it might also involve taking more extreme measures, such as providing the plant with UV light for a specific number of hours per day or a special mixture of fertilizer to keep a plant healthy.

Why container gardening works

Container gardening works because gardeners are able to reproduce all of the conditions plants need to grow. Within the container, gardeners can provide the plant with the right soil type, specific nutrients the plant needs, and the right amount of water and sunlight it requires. Gardeners can give the plants enough space so that the air circulation keeps plant diseases at bay.

If those needed conditions are not available naturally outdoors or in a windowsill inside the home, gardeners can reproduce them with UV lights, humidifiers, trellises, and other devices that trick the plant into thinking it is growing on the floor of an African jungle, a sand dune in Tunisia, or any other habitat where the plant originated.

Space Constraints

Apartments, patio homes, and other homes that have little or no outdoor space in which to grow plants can still be graced with green living things by starting an indoor garden. Containers can fit in windowsills, on bookshelves, and on dressers and can be stacked along baker's racks and otherwise fit into the usable space of an apartment or small house.

A baker's rack is a particularly useful way to fit a large number of plants into a tiny space. These racks have short wire shelves that allow plenty of light to plants on lower shelves. They also allow for maximum air circulation around the plants. Even the smallest indoor space or balcony can fit a four- or five-shelf baker's rack in an unused corner.

Easy Portability

Many gardening fans want to grow plants that are unable to survive the climate in their area. Container gardening is a way to grow the type of plants you desire and allow them to survive when cold weather arrives or extreme heat plagues your area. With an outdoor container, plants can easily be brought indoors or outdoors when the weather changes.

Many plants that will be grown outside can start indoors in containers. Planting seeds or nurturing seedlings indoors in the winter gives the plants a head start on the growing season when spring comes. This means a longer growing season and more fruits or vegetables for the gardener to enjoy.

Ideal for renters or temporary residents

In some cases, gardeners do not want to invest the time, money, and materials that growing plants requires in a place they will live only for a short period. With container gardening, you can still grow the plants you want without having to leave them behind when you move, ensuring your time, effort, and money will not go to waste. Renters who do not intend to stay in a home long term, those who move often for their jobs, or college students who move yearly can plant in containers and take their plants along with them to their next adventure.

Bringing your container garden with you when you move is often a welcome sense of continuity during a hectic time. Although you cannot take that oak tree, you can take all of your beautiful flowers, your herb plants, and your little produce garden.

Ideal for growing food between seasons

When growing any type of plant, you must take into account the temperature needs of the plant. In some areas, there are many weeks of in-between time, when temperatures vary greatly from day to night. Container gardening makes it easier to grow the plants outdoors when the temperature is favorable and bring the plants indoors when it is not.

For some regions, temperatures vary during much of the year. Very dry regions often have high temperature variations between day and night, which makes it difficult to get consistent results with outdoor plants. Moving the plants inside each night can become a step in your routine for caring for the plant.

Inhospitable Terrain

Many of the plants we grow are simply not suited for the area in which we want to grow them. An area that has sandy topsoil will not contain the organic materials needed to grow most fruits and vegetables. The topsoil is the top layer of soil — generally about 2 inches in depth — and contains a high level of organic material. A yard with large rocks just under the soil can literally take years to clear in anticipation of a crop of flowers, herbs, and produce plants. Preparing a container of potting soil to grow these plants is infinitely easier and less time consuming than treating large areas of topsoil with fertilizer mixtures or removing large areas of rocks from your yard.

Too much or not enough sun

The amount of sun a plant gets is perhaps the most important factor in how healthy the plant will be. Every plant has its own light needs, and those needs cannot be changed to match the outdoor environment. For plants that need dappled light, a filtered sunlight condition that leaves spots of light on the plants and ground below, or partial shade, living in an area with no shade and direct sunlight will result in a shriveled, miserable plant. Moving these plants inside in the afternoon can determine whether a plant lives or dies. A container allows you to easily accomplish this.

Conversely, living in a wooded area that provides constant shade is not the ideal environment for a plant that requires full sunlight. Growing the plant indoors in a container is possible with the careful use of windows and sun lamps. Such aids give you the chance to grow exotic plants that originated across the world.

Plants that require full sunlight generally need it for at least six hours each day. If a home does not have a single outdoor area or a window that provides full sunlight for the required time frame, you might have to move the container plant from one outdoor area to another or from one indoor window to another several times in one day.

To recreate full sunlight conditions where none exist, make a note of where the sunlight falls, and record how long it stays in that position each day. If one outdoor area gets two hours of full sun and another gets four hours of sun, one quick daily move can deliver all the sunlight the plant needs.

To recreate partial shade conditions, only expose the place to full sunlight for two to four hours each day. To do this, you might opt to leave the plant outdoors for a few hours each day and keep it inside the rest of the time. An indoor plant can be placed in a sunny windowsill for a few hours each day to get all the sunlight it needs. Finding a place that gets only a certain amount of sunlight each day and placing the plant there will make this process even easier.

Some plants actually require neither full sun nor shade. Dappled light is required for plants such as chervil, Corsican mint, and lily of the valley. Plants that need dappled light can burn under direct light and will fail to grow well in the shade. A plant that requires dappled light needs special placement to recreate that lighting condition. Outdoors, the container can be placed under a small tree to give it the small spots of light that dappled-light plants need. Trees with thin leaves, such as birch trees, can create dappled lighting conditions. Indoors, the plant might need to be placed behind other plants that receive full sunlight. This recreates the natural dappling that the plant would have from a tree outdoors.

Purple daisies in dappled light.

Too hot or too cold

Like the lighting situation, the temperature of the air and the soil is important to the growth and health of the plant. Indoor environments are far easier to control than outdoor ones, and keeping plants indoors in containers makes it possible to control the exact temperature of the plant.

It also makes it possible to keep plants alive that would have died outdoors during the winter. Plants that thrive in very specific temperature zones might sustain damage from a day with unusually hot or cold temperatures. During a heat or cold wave, those plants might die altogether. The same plant, when in a container, could simply be whisked indoors for a little TLC instead of left outdoors to brave the temperatures.

When keeping plants indoors, remember that rooms have hot and cold spots caused by air registers and windows. When placing a plant that has very specific temperature needs, use a thermometer to measure the temperature of the area where the plant will be placed. That area could be very different from the average temperature of the house. A windowsill that gets full sunlight all day might still be too cold for the plant if the cold air from the winter weather outside is leaking into the room.

Using a greenhouse can also create a different environment for container plants. In cold climates, a greenhouse can create higher temperatures by trapping the heat from the sun and creating a different environment than the one outdoors.

Too much or not enough rain

Like the temperature outdoors, the amount of rainfall is not under your control. Watering plants with a hose or other irrigation system is one solution, but plants that need a great deal of water will require plenty of time and attention that many gardeners cannot spare. Watering often with a hose can also lead to fungal infections in plants. Irrigation systems that use drip watering to wet the soil can be expensive and difficult to install. A drip-watering system uses a drip line to add water slowly at ground level. Drip-watering systems for potted plants add water at the soil level.

By growing water-loving plants in containers, water put into the container will remain longer than if the water was applied to the ground. The ingredients in potting soil allow it to retain more water than natural soil and for a longer period of time than in-ground soil. The barrier of the container also means that the water will not be absorbed by the neighboring soil or evaporate quickly. This means less watering time is required and you have a better chance of keeping the soil moist long term. *For more information on types of containers, see Chapter 3.*

Being able to water container plants from the bottom is also helpful for keeping fungal infections at bay. The pot of a water-loving plant can be placed into a larger container of water on top of a dish containing water. This allows the plant's soil to absorb the water from the bottom up, avoiding wet leaves. Outdoors, this is a quick fix for plants that are not getting enough rainfall. Indoors, it is a timesaver that means less time spent watering plants each day.

Apartment or condo dwellers might not have any "ground" to plant in

Many dwellers of apartments and condos dream of being able to grow their own food and cultivate their own flowers. With container gardening, this does not have to remain just a wish. Even tiny apartments or condos have enough space for a few small container-grown plants.

In addition, apartment and condo dwellers might have outdoor space to grow plants beyond their own specific patch of ground. Terraces and balconies are ideal places to create a small container garden that produces both beauty and your own produce and herbs. In some areas, fire escapes are often used to house container plants, but you should know that in many places, this practice is illegal because it presents a fire hazard. Rooftops also present a useful place for placing containers and growing food and flowers.

Aesthetic Appeal

In addition to all of the practical reasons for growing plants in containers, there are a large number of aesthetic ones as well. Containers come in so many shapes, sizes, and colors that they can easily become home décor. They can add a bit of color, elegance, or quirky style to a home. Outdoors, they present an opportunity to personalize the area around the home.

Container gardens also present a challenge to your creativity. There is no need to stick to standard terra-cotta pots or purchase the latest plastic ones for your container plants. Almost anything can be used as a container for a plant — from an old work boot to a gallon jug that you want to reuse. People who want to live a "green" lifestyle can use recycled items as containers for planting.

For collectors, finding a container that matches their favorite collectible items can be a thrilling acquisition. For example, people who love country kitchen décor can use a rooster planter to hold kitchen herbs. People who collect model trains can find planters shaped like train cars.

Easily change the look of the yard or accommodate different events

If you love to change your home décor often, container gardening makes it possible to do so on a mass scale. You can change the containers to match the season or complement your latest color scheme. Holiday containers can be used as a part of your holiday décor, or you can change containers as your personal tastes morph.

For events, get-togethers, and other occasions, your containers can be changed, moved, or accessorized. If you have a balcony full of container plants and want to fill it with people for an event, just haul the containers inside for the evening. If you want your guests greeted by cheery décor, place large, colorful containers near the entrance of your home to set the mood for your guests.

Decorate specific areas that might not be equipped to sustain in-ground plants

Some yards have one stubborn area where nothing seems to grow. If you love gardening and have a yard that shows off your cultivating skills, this spot stands out even more. The area might be rocky, it might have too much shade, or it might just enjoy taunting you, but by placing a container over it, you can hide the spot with a growing, flourishing plant.

Some yards have one or more areas that have poor drainage. Those areas generally cannot support plant life because of the drainage requirements of most plants. Fruit, vegetable, and berry plants must be grown in an area that has good drainage to keep the roots, leaves, and fruits or vegetables from rotting or developing fungal infections.

Place a large container in this area to fully utilize the extra water. This area of your yard can be dressed up with a large flowering bush or used to grow more of your edibles. If the entire yard has drainage issues, use many plant containers of various sizes to create a garden or a flower bed.

For Food

Having herbs, fruits, and vegetables handy is a constant need for every family. The logistics of keeping fresh produce and herbs in the house, though, can often be challenging. Many times shoppers buy a large load of produce only to have it go bad before their families have eaten it. Even though it is a constant need, produce simply cannot be stockpiled. Fruits and vegetables do not stay fresh for long after they have been picked.

Going to the grocery store a few times a week to buy these nutritious foods takes more time and effort than most people are willing to devote to fresh produce, even if they are passionate about having it in the house. Instead, consider growing produce at home, ready whenever your family needs or wants it. With fresh produce in the house, kids can pick themselves a nutritious snack instead of turning to unhealthy junk food. Growing your own food gives your family access to fresh produce throughout much of the year.

Growing some of the family's food can also be an educational experience for children by showing them how their food is created. They can see the work that goes into growing food and that hard work does produce enjoyable results. Families might enjoy tending their container garden together, spending time learning about the different plants and nurturing them together.

Save money at the grocery store

The economic realities of keeping fresh produce and herbs in the house are another logistical problem for many families. The weekly budget for fresh foods might be small because of the limited buying power your budget has when purchasing these expensive items. Pound for pound, a family's food budget will go further when they buy processed or canned foods instead of buying fresh, ripe produce and herbs.

Many homes suffer from a lack of fresh foods due to the temptation to buy cheaper options. In some families, it is not a matter of choice; buying enough food for everyone in the household each week might mean not buying fresh produce. By setting aside money for a few simple gardening supplies instead, families can slash the weekly grocery budget and still have the herbs and produce they need.

Always have a ready supply of fresh, nutrient-dense produce

Vegetables are some of the most nutrient-dense foods available. When they are boiled and processed, they lose many of those nutrients. Canned produce is known to be less nutrient-dense than fresh fruit and vegetables. According to WebMD, the cooking process used for canned produce results in a loss of vitamins, such as vitamin C and thiamine. Canned peas have 73 percent less vitamin C than fresh peas and 80 percent less thiamine. Growing produce items at home ensures your vegetables will not lose their nutrients.

Growing food in containers also means having a variety of fresh, nutritious food available when temptation strikes. Instead of snacking on a bowl of chips, your family will be more likely to grab a succulent cucumber or melon growing nearby. This can change a family's mind about what to eat, which often means healthier eating habits for everyone in the household.

Know where your food is coming from and what has been used to produce it

Many consumers prefer organic food, but it costs more to produce commercially and, therefore, costs more at the grocery store. Without the use of pesticides and herbicides, food grown on a large scale will not yield as much as chemically treated plants.

Even if you choose to pay more for organic food at the grocery store, your produce might still have been treated with herbicides and pesticides. Organic simply means the pesticides used were created naturally instead of synthesized. Certified organic foods can be treated with organic pesticides and organic herbicides, some of which are harmful chemicals much like the synthetic versions.

Eating organic food whenever possible can be expensive, and organic food can sometimes be in short supply. Lower crop yields and market demands for cheap food mean organic food usually has little shelf space among the other food available — which results in a small selection for consumers.

When you grow your own edible items at home, you are in control of what goes into them and what is used to grow them. You can grow them as organically as you choose, using organic pesticides and herbicides or no pesticides at all. Edible items grown indoors often need no chemical interference except the occasional organic fertilizer for the soil.

Being more self-sufficient is a very real need for some container gardeners. Weathering a crop shortage or recall that leaves you without your favorite produce may be enough to make you want to grow your own, but there are many other advantages of being more self-sufficient.

A major disaster might make it impossible to purchase food for days or even weeks at a time. Past disasters such as earthquakes, hurricanes, and ice storms prevented people from buying food at a grocery store for many days. When you grow your own produce at home, you do not have to worry about being left without food for an extended amount of time.

CASE STUDY: GROWING INDOORS VERSUS OUTDOORS

Jeff Dahlberg
Cheap Seeds, owner
Jeff@cheapseeds.com
www.cheapseeds.com

I grow flowers and vegetables in pots, boots, hanging baskets, birdhouses, tires, real beds, and an occasional toilet just for fun. My first memory of planting seeds in a pot is from when I was six years old. That would make me a 49-year veteran. I have loved every minute of it.

I sell seeds to many people in my business. So many people just do not have the space for a garden. People have sent me pictures of balconies that are just packed with vegetables and flowers growing in containers. It is amazing how much they can fit on a balcony of 6-by-4 feet.

The main advantages to growing vegetables and flowers in containers are that gardeners can move them in and out of the sun and find just the right amount of sunlight the plants need to grow well. Gardeners can have vegetables growing inside during the summer and winter. And believe me, it is so good to have fresh herbs and vegetables in the winter.

Gardeners can fill in an outdoor garden with a few pots to make it look just right.

Gardeners can grow just about any type of plant in a container indoors and give it just the right amount of light, humidity, and soil. Gardeners can plant fruit trees out of the zone in which they should be grown and then bring them inside their garage for the winter.

People choose to grow food indoors because it tastes better than what you buy at the store, it is easy to do, it is much cheaper, it can be done all year long, and it is fun for the kids.

The main problems with indoor container gardening are that lights might be needed to grow some types of plants, space is limited, and large vining vegetables are hard to grow inside. Gardeners must make sure the containers do not dry out.

I usually grow several types of herbs in a south-facing window. I grow a couple of tomato plants under the lights with some leaf lettuce and radishes around the tomatoes. In the summer, I have a big garden so I can grow a lot of vegetables. If I did not have that, I would grow more inside.

Inside, the best plants to grow in containers are flowers, tomatoes, lettuce, herbs, radishes, mushrooms, carrots, and peas. Outside, you can grow any flowers, any vegetables, some types of trees, and many bulbs.

Today, people are into growing their own food to save money and because it has a better, fresher taste. It is also safer and easy to do. No plants I have tried grow poorly in containers.

Pests that can be a problem in an indoor garden are spider mites, thrips, and fungus gnats. Without using pesticides, gardeners can get rid of pests by using diatomaceous earth and neem oil.

Chapter 2

WHAT SHOULD I GROW?

Deciding which plants to grow is often the fun part of container gardening. The thousands of plants that can grow in containers give you endless possibilities for your garden. Looking through seed catalogs and at the plants available in nurseries will introduce you to plants you never knew existed. Container gardening can make each season a new adventure as you try new plants and taste new fruits and vegetables.

Grow Plants that are Well-Adapted to Your Environmental Conditions and Weather

The easiest plants to grow are ones whose needs match your native climate. If you plan to grow your plants indoors, this might not be a factor in your decision about what to grow, but if the plants will be grown outdoors, it should be. Although you can compensate some things, such as low rainfall, cold daytime temperatures, and little sunlight, do not expect to be able to grow sunflowers or other sun-loving plants that require warmth. Hot places that get little rain will not be able to grow water-loving plants outdoors where the water will evaporate quickly, even if the plant is in a container.

Although it might be tempting to grow something completely unsuited to your environment, your success rate will be lower. Remember that your windows will provide the majority of the sunlight for your plants if you grow indoors. The area around windows might be cold in the winter if you live in a cold climate.

Plants grow longer indoors during the winter than they do outside, but their growth is slower, and some plants are dormant until the weather warms. Although moving a plant indoors during cold nights and winter months will allow them to live longer, vegetable plants will not produce vegetables throughout the winter.

Grow Plants that Suit Your USDA Hardiness Zone

Outdoor container growing should be planned with the help of the USDA Plant Hardiness Zone Map, available at **www.usna.usda.gov/Hardzone/ushzmap.html**. *A copy of the map is also included in Appendix A of this book.* The climate zones across the United States have been delineated into 11 different zones, depending on the average minimum temperature of each area. The zones twist and turn and sometimes form small zone islands in order to represent the exact temperature information for that area.

The minimum temperature the area can expect is a good indicator of which plants will grow in that area. Although some of the zones do not seem to differ greatly in the minimum temperature indication, even a few degrees can make a huge difference to outdoor plants.

Each USDA Plant Hardiness Zone is represented by a number and a color on the official map. To use the chart, find the zone covering your location. Do not rely on simply estimating by using your state's name or your position within the state. Each state has many different zones within it, and your specific area might be rated with a different zone than other parts of the state or even nearby counties.

Study the zone map to find your specific location. Your location might be in the middle of a zone and easy to find or it might be on the cusp of two zones. If that is the case, study the map to determine exactly where your home is located. Once you find the right spot, compare the color of that area to the color-coded key at the bottom of the map. An online ZIP code zone finder can be helpful. Although the USDA does not have a ZIP code reference on their website, sites such as GardenWeb (**www.gardenweb.com**) do.

When purchasing seedlings or plant seeds, know your zone number and check the USDA zone marked on the tag or container if the plant will be housed outdoors for any length of time. The zones listed on the plant tag or seed packet will usually indicate a range of zones rather than just one zone number. If the plant will be kept outdoors, the zone range must include your zone. If you buy a plant online or from a catalog that is not already planted in soil, look up the USDA zone for the plant online or in the reference section of this book to find out whether it has a chance of surviving in your climate. Even receiving the plant in the mail can result in the death of that plant if the zones do not align.

Grow Plants You Enjoy Eating

If you want to grow edible produce, make sure that your efforts will go toward something you actually want to eat. Buying a seedling because it sounds like it would grow an interesting vegetable is a gamble that might end in wasted time and money. A gardener who grows 10 pounds of potatoes in containers might be a successful container gardener, but if the gardener hates potatoes, it all will have been for nothing. Growing plants that you dislike can make gardening seem like a chore instead of a way to produce the items you love and want to eat.

If you want to grow a few new and interesting items, take a trip to the grocery store to conduct research. A taste test might result in the discovery of many new flavors you never knew existed. Browse through the produce section and buy a small sample of produce items that look interesting or that you know to be high in nutrition. Peruse the spice aisle to find a few herbs you are not familiar with. Take the food home and taste test each one. Write out a list of the items you would like to grow at home to enjoy again, and make sure they can be grown in your zone if you plan to grow them outdoors. Let your family members taste test the items as well. If you have children, being able to grow produce they like can mean the difference between excitement about the project and healthier eating habits and indifference toward your growing efforts.

Another way to determine which items to grow is to look up recipes that sound tasty and then browse through the ingredients. Most recipes contain some herbs or vegetables you can grow at home. Look up recipes you could not cook in the past because the ingredients were a little exotic or out of your price range.

Grow foods you already like and new variations of old favorites

Many of the items you want to grow are favorites you have eaten many times. You may choose to grow tomatoes because you use them frequently in your cooking and lemons because you love them in your tea. Consider what other members of the household will enjoy eating. If you have kids at home, think about the nutritious fruits and vegetables they already like and are familiar with. By growing fruits and vegetables everyone is fond of, you can boost the nutrition levels of home-cooked meals.

Growing your own plants can give you the opportunity to try new and exotic variations of your favorites. If you love red tomatoes, try a purple,

Organic purple and yellow heirloom tomatoes

striped variety. If you like snacking on carrots, grow tiny specialty carrots or carrots of the white, yellow, or purple variety.

If there are fruits and vegetables you do not care for, there might be other varieties you do like. Although you might not enjoy red tomatoes, there are countless other varieties of tomatoes with different flavors. Lollipop tomatoes have a lemony flavor that might appeal more to your tastes. During your taste test, sample different varieties of the foods you are unsure about. You might discover that, though you do not care for most beans, there is a variety that is nutritious and tasty.

Some of the more exotic flavors might not be available at your local grocery store. Heirloom varieties, which are older varieties that have not been developed for commercial purposes, are rarely carried in grocery stores. If you are thinking of growing heirloom plants, you might need to grow the plant for a season to find out whether it suits your tastes.

White, orange, and purple carrots.

Grow Plants that Work Well in Containers

St. John's wort

If a plant is not suited for container living, no amount of care will produce a thriving plant. A plant that needs an enormous amount of soil will not work well in most containers or planters. Some plants do not like to be transplanted and often do not survive the process. Re-potting these plants into new containers when they outgrow their current container can result in the loss of the plants before they have produced their fruit or vegetables. If you are growing a plant that does not like to be transplanted, such as carrots or lettuce, the plant can still do well in a container as long as care is taken to start it in a large enough container. With the right-sized container, re-potting with growth will be unnecessary.

What type of plant works well in containers?

Before choosing the plants you will grow in your containers, it is important to find out the conditions they require for optimum growth and how large the resulting plants

Blooming chives

will be. The best types of container plants are ones that grow quickly and stay compact.

Succulents, desert plants that store water in their leaves and stems, generally grow well in containers and need little care once planted. Berries, tomatoes, peas, squash, and small citrus fruit trees thrive well in containers as long as the containers are large enough to contain the roots. Most small flowering plants will grow well in containers as long as the lighting, temperature, and soil conditions are right.

Virtually any herb will grow well in a container. The compact size of most herbs lends itself to the use of containers. Many larger herbs, such as evening primrose and St. John's wort, began as wildflowers. This origin means they are hardy and need little care or special attention. Smaller herbs, such as chamomile and chives, are small enough to be tucked in small spaces throughout the house that aid in their growth and health, including windowsills.

What type of plant does not grow well in containers?

Large plants that need plenty of spreading room either above or below the soil generally are not practical for container gardening. Trees with large root balls, which is the entire root system of the plant, such as orange trees and apple trees, will not grow well in containers. Plants that have very deep roots or that grow to large heights, such as flowering maples, some varieties of morning glories, and dogwoods, can be impractical for containers. Tall, heavy plants, such as olive trees and bamboo, will make the containers hard to move, and plants with large, thick roots, such as juniper and holly, will be too cramped by the container to allow for the needed plant growth. Potatoes need wide spaces in which to grow, and even a large outdoor planter might not be large enough.

Cauliflower and sprouting broccoli are sprawling plants that can be difficult to grow in containers. Pumpkins are plants that produce large, heavy vegetables, which makes them an impractical container choice. Sweet corn is another plant that needs space a container cannot provide.

Although some small trees, such as lemon and lime trees, do grow well in containers, a large tree with a thick trunk will have an enormous root ball. These trees are not well-suited for growing in containers. In general, check the mature size of a tree by reading the plant's tag or the seed packet. Plants more than 3 feet in height can be awkward to carry and can develop thick stems that make the plant difficult to move and transplant.

Grow Plants that Complement Your Garden or Décor

One of the aesthetic principles of gardening is to grow items that complement each other. The color, size, and shape of the items might be a consideration for you if your goal is to grow ornamental plants. The texture of the leaves, the complexity of the flowers, and the smell of the plant might also be important considerations.

Your outdoor container plants can be planned by creating a basic color scheme. Some people prefer similar colors, such as blue and purple, grouped together. You might prefer to have as many colors as possible to dazzle guests with bright, eye-catching colors. Some gardeners choose a single color and only grow ornamental plants that bloom in that color. Choosing plants of varying heights for a flower garden is often done because it makes it easier to see the plants and gives the garden, as a whole, depth and visual interest.

An additional benefit to container gardening, the color of the containers also factors into the garden's theme. Use the containers to add additional splashes of color, or choose neutral-colored containers so the containers do not interfere with the colors of the blooms. Choose bright containers to draw attention to drab-looking plants. Also, pick the same color pot for all of your plants to unify the look of the container garden.

Planting a large container with multiple plants

One way to fill containers is to plant multiple plants in the same container. This is made easier with large containers or planters, but even

smaller containers can be used in this way. The size of the plants and their potential widths are the most important factors when choosing the plants and containers for this type of container gardening.

Using several different plants in the same container is a way of creating a small garden within one container. The same principle of plant choice in a garden with multiple containers can be used when choosing plants to be grown in a single container. Group

similar plants together or plants that bloom in different colors together to add contrast and visual interest.

Nurseries that sell multiple plants in one container usually pot plants in a pattern. Many of the mixed-plant containers are arranged with one tall plant, one smaller plant that has dense foliage, and one plant that provides a ground cover for the soil.

With this arrangement, the entire surface of the container is covered in vegetation, and the varied height of the plants gives the arrangement depth that makes it more visually appealing. A plant arrangement that includes one or more flowering plants can be done on a large scale, with a large container covered in different-colored blooms, or on a tiny scale, with a few small flowers to draw the eye to the arrangement.

For example, planting English ivy, marigolds, and creeping thyme together in a single container results in the tall, dense, and covered combination. This grouping will provide wide foliage from the creeping thyme, which covers the soil, bright color from the marigolds, and a tall climber in the English ivy to add height.

Another combination is ornamental grass to add soil cover and rosemary to add a little height. Many types of rosemary can be shaped into tall, thin columns or tall, cone-shaped arrangements. Then, add a Pothos — a fast-growing green plant — to add depth, and you have a complete, living plant arrangement that has visual appeal and provides the useful herb rosemary for cooking.

Grow Plants You Can Maintain

Once you have narrowed down the list of plants that you are interested in growing, take a critical look at the amount of care that each plant requires. If you know you do not want fussy plants that need a good deal of attention, consider this before buying seeds or seedlings. A plant might be beautiful, and it might grow a type of food you love, but if you do not have the time and equipment to grow it, avoid it.

Some plants are easy to grow and do not require much attention, and others need plenty of dedicated care. The type you choose to grow is up to you and should fit in well with your lifestyle.

Consider your gardening budget when deciding which plants to grow. If you are on a tight budget and need to garden as inexpensively as possible, avoid choosing plants that need heat lamps, grow lights, and/or humidifiers. Instead, choose plants that grow well in your local climate.

Know your time constraints

When deciding which plants to grow and how many to grow at once, consider the amount of time you have to devote to gardening. A house filled with container plants that need extensive care but do not get it will soon become a house full of *dead* plants. If you have little time, consider starting slowly with two or three plants to make sure you have the time to adequately take care of a container garden.

Think critically about how much time you have to devote to your plants. If your plants must be moved in and out of the home regularly, consider the amount of time it will take to do this. If you choose water-loving plants, consider how much time it will take to check the soil for moisture and water the plants.

If you have plenty of time to spare, you still might not wish to spend it in the care of your plants. If you know you prefer to spend your leisure time away from gardening and might neglect your plants, choose plants that require little from you.

Which plants require little maintenance?

As mentioned, some plants need very little care. These plants rarely need to be fertilized, if at all, and they will not have finicky light, temperature, and humidity requirements. The following are a few plants that are easy to care for:

- **Christmas cactus:** This plant is a compact succulent that needs little care from its owner. It doesn't require much water and tolerates most humidity levels. It can be kept in a small container and in light levels from low to high. It will bloom in the winter with pink or red flowers.

- **Peace lilies:** These bushy flowering plants are slow growing and do not need much light. They are not finicky about humidity levels and do not need special fertilization. Plain potting soil and weekly watering will keep them alive for decades.

- **Russian sage:** With full sunlight and regular watering, this plant will provide you with a profuse display of lavender flowers that grow on tall spikes.

- **African violet:** Water these plants approximately twice a week and re-pot them once a year to accommodate their growing size. African violets will tolerate indirect sunlight, direct sunlight, partial shade, and full sunlight. The only regular maintenance you need to provide — other than watering — is to pinch off the dead flowers when necessary.

- **Siberian iris:** These plants require moist soil but little other care. They are not picky about their soil and are tolerant of drought. They are also beautiful in color and have large, showy flowers.

- **Surecrop   strawberry:** These strawberry plants will grow as long as they are being watered. The name "surecrop" was chosen because this variety is especially easy to grow and a good yield can always be expected. These plants are hardy and need little care to yield strawberries.

- **French beans:** French beans grow as tall as 8 feet high and produce multitudes of tasty beans. Although the plants do need to be supported with a trellis or tall stakes, they need little care once the preliminary work is done. The containers need to be 18 inches in diameter or larger in order to accommodate the mature plants. Keep the soil moist, and the plants will continue to produce beans.

- **Lettuce:** Lettuce is a fast-maturing vegetable that requires little care. Most lettuce varieties go from seeds to harvest in less than two months. When planting lettuce, keep the soil moist.

- **Onions:** Onions are compact plants that are resistant to insects and tolerant of most soil types. They are resilient to freezes and most plant diseases. Provide the plants with consistent moisture and make sure the soil drains well, and the plants will produce onions.

- **Swiss chard:** This vegetable is one of the easiest to grow. It is tolerant of cold weather and resistant to most plant diseases and insects. It matures quickly, usually in less than two months, and tolerates most types of soil.

- **Mint:** Most mint plants are resistant to disease and grow well even when little care is provided. Because these plants thrive even with less attention, they are considered an invasive weed by many gardeners.

- **Rosemary:** Rosemary is another plant that grows so well that it can become invasive if not kept pruned and confined to a pot. Rosemary flourishes as long as it is watered regularly, and it resists most pests.

Which plants require a lot of maintenance?

A finicky plant will require more attention in regards to sunlight, temperature, and water conditions than a more tolerant plant. Plants that require a good deal of maintenance are often difficult for beginning gardeners to grow and include:

- **Gardenias:** Gardenias are fussy about their soil, and they need high humidity levels. If you do not live in a very humid area, you will need to purchase a humidifier to make the air in the room more humid. This might also require closing off a room to keep the humidity inside. Gardenias are also susceptible to a long list of parasites and plant diseases and must be inspected often.

- **Indian paintbrush:** This beautiful plant with bright, spiky flowers is admired by many, but it is a difficult plant to grow. Successfully growing this plant involves providing a host plant in which the paintbrush can feed. Its parasitic nature means planting it near other plants can lead to the death of those plants.

- **Citrus fruit trees:** The unique growing conditions of these small trees and bushes can be difficult to reproduce in other climates. Key lime and lemon trees can be particularly difficult to grow outside of Florida and California. Although full sun is needed to grow these trees, necessitating plenty of outdoor time, an unexpected freeze can kill them quickly.

- **Apple trees:** Apple trees need several trees present in order to cross-pollinate. Without at least one other apple tree nearby, the tree will never produce apples. A single apple tree may also die sooner and grow poorly. Indoor apple growers might not have the space needed to grow several apple trees in the house. Even when growing outdoors, re-potting multiple apple trees can be prohibitively difficult.

- **Pumpkins:** Pumpkins are extremely finicky about the amount of water and sunlight they need. They can be difficult for even experienced gardeners to grow because of the specialized soil nutrients they need throughout their lifetime.

CASE STUDY: WHY GROW IN CONTAINERS?

Johanna De Rosa
derosajohanna@yahoo.com.au
Phone: 61 08 9439 3236

I have grown a wide range of plants in containers in the hot, dry Mediterranean climate of Perth, Australia. I have used container gardening to grow fruits and vegetables, as well as ornamental plants; I also use container gardening as a way of nursing plants before I am ready to plant them out in their eventual location.

In my climate, one advantage to container gardening is being able to keep plants in a preferred location depending on the weather. During our summers, many plants simply would not do well, or survive, in the hot sun or an exposed situation. I like to use protected, shaded areas for certain plants during this part of the year. Then, when the heat of summer is over, the container plants can be moved to a sunny, warm location.

Aside from the convenience of having a food plant located in or near the kitchen where food is prepared, some food plants are simply not suited for growing outdoors in some locations. Using containers indoors increases the number of choices that a gardener has when it comes to what plants can be grown successfully in their location.

The major problems with indoor container gardening are mess, drainage, and light. Some preparation and planning is needed to find a solution to these issues.

The number of plants that are generally manageable to house indoors completely depends on what you want from your container gardening and how much room, time, and effort you are prepared to devote to it. Some people prefer to keep a small herb garden only, while others grow many larger-sized ornamental plants, such as varieties of palms, ferns, and bamboos.

Container gardening is especially good for some plants that require specific soil and drainage conditions. Examples would be acid-loving plants, such as gardenias, camellias, and azaleas. Slower-growing or smaller-sized plants tend to be most suitable, unless you are prepared to re-pot a vigorous plant frequently as it outgrows its container.

Very large-growing or vigorous plants are not the most suitable for container gardening. In terms of their early life, before they take off and outgrow their container, I have rarely seen a plant that is absolutely unsuitable for container gardening. Given the right soil mix or growing medium and correct drainage as well as other conditions, almost any plant can be grown in a container until it becomes too large.

The rising cost of fresh food is a major motivator for many who have begun to grow plants for food. Other great advantages include knowing exactly how your food has been grown, where it came from, and what chemicals were or were not involved in the production of your food. In my area at least, organic fruits and vegetables are much more cheaply produced at home than bought at stores.

The advantages of growing your own food include cutting costs, knowing what conditions your food has been exposed to, knowing where it came from, knowing whether it was produced responsibly, and knowing what impact the production of your food has had on the environment.

Pest problems are generally minimal in an indoor garden. Sometimes a bigger problem is a lack of beneficial or symbiotic organisms, which may be less likely to live indoors.

Many pests can be hand-removed, sprayed off with water, or controlled with simple, natural remedies that can be made at home. Many natural or non-chemical pest control methods can also be found at garden stores or specialty nurseries.

Chapter 3

CHOOSING AND PREPARING CONTAINERS FOR GROWING

Many factors go into choosing containers for your plants, which range from the look of the containers to the composition, size, and shape of each. Some people delight in choosing beautiful containers that reflect their personal taste and the décor of their homes. Other people want their containers to be as functional as possible without much thought to the colors or shapes of the pots.

Size Matters

In practical terms, the size of the container is the most important factor of all. A plant that does not have enough room for its root ball will not grow well and might not produce the flowers, herbs, or produce you desire.

When in doubt about which size container to purchase, as a general rule, always buy the larger pot.

At least 1 to 2 inches of space around the root ball is needed to allow the roots of a plant to re-pot successfully. The roots need to spread out in their new pot. If the roots are too concentrated within the soil, they cannot take in nutrients efficiently. A plant that runs out of room for its expanding roots will soon have serious health problems. Its roots will dry up, grow incorrectly, and stop nourishing the plant. Once this happens, it will be difficult to save the plant.

Tiny pots are often chosen for planting new seeds or holding tiny seedlings as they are being separated from a seed-starting tray. The tiny pots can house the seedlings until an appropriate container is chosen for them. This allows you to choose the strongest of the seedlings and select those to transplant into a larger pot. When choosing a pot for transplanting, consider the adult size of the plant. If the plant is a slow-growing one, you might choose to re-pot it approximately every six months to accommodate growth. For fast-growing plants, choose a pot large enough to hold the mature plant so it does not need to be transplanted many times.

Although you will not see your plant's roots every day, they are an extremely important part of the plant. Every plant needs to have room to expand its roots, and it must have enough soil around those roots to allow the roots to draw in the moisture and nutrients it needs.

If the plant has a large surface area, you also need a pot with a wide surface area at the top. Most plant pots are slightly wider at the top than they are at the bottom, and the depth of the pot is usually the same as the top width. When purchasing a pot, know the size designation given is the size of the top diameter measurement. Seedlings are also sold with this pot measurement rather than the measurement of the plant itself. When you purchase a 6-inch plant, this means the plant is currently in a pot that is 6 inches wide at the top and 6 inches deep. You should have a container that is at least 10 inches to re-pot the plant after it is purchased.

Containers are generally used to allow the plant to be moved when needed. If the plant, soil, and pot are too heavy to be moved, this can negate the whole purpose of growing the plant in the container. If you choose a very large pot and want it to be portable, be sure to choose one that is not made from a heavy material. If you choose a heavy material and anticipate having problems moving the pot later, you can place the container onto rollers before filling it to allow it to be moved no matter how heavy the contents eventually become.

Container Composition

There is no reason to discount any one material for all needs. Different materials have different uses in container gardening, and some will likely appeal to you and work better with your gardening plan than others. You might choose to have a container garden made up of many different types of containers, or you might fall in love with one type and want only that type for all of your potted plants.

Plastic

Plastic has several features that can make it useful as a plant container. The first of these is plastic is light-weight. Even a large pot can be moved with ease if it is made from plastic. Plastic containers also seal in moisture that can leak out of more porous plant pot materials, such as clay.

Plastic is so versatile that it can be used to create any number of shapes, colors, and designs. This makes it easy to find a plastic pot to fit any décor.

Some people view plastic as a poor-quality material because it is often less expensive than other materials, and if you like a more traditional look, plastic might not be for you.

Clay

Clay plant containers have been used for as long as people have been placing plants into pots. The first cultivated indoor plant was likely placed into a clay pot. Clay can be created in a variety of thicknesses and decorated with paints of any color.

The traditional look of clay makes it a perennial favorite among container gardeners, but there are also disadvantages to using clay. The porous nature of clay allows moisture to leak through the sides of the container, which makes it difficult to keep the soil damp for long.

Some gardeners like clay containers so much that they start making their own clay pots. This can be a fun hobby that will give you the exact sizes and shapes you need and can provide a means of self-expression and creativity.

Concrete

Concrete is a heavy material that can make medium and large containers difficult to move around, but there are some advantages to using it. A small concrete pot is less likely to be knocked over during storms. Concrete is also plentiful and very inexpensive, which makes large pots more affordable.

If you want to create new plant containers out of recycled materials, there are always concrete blocks around that can be used as planters. Planting with concrete blocks might not be the most attractive way to plant, but it is cheap and keeps the blocks from being thrown away.

Wood

Wood is a classic pot material that goes with most home décors. Wood makes beautiful, large planting containers for the larger plants kept outdoors, but the heavy nature of these wooden containers makes them difficult to transport. They are often put into one spot and kept there indefinitely because of their weight.

Although wooden containers are among the most attractive, they do not hold up very well over time. The moisture needed for the plant inside will eventually rot the wooden container. If the pot is kept indoors, it might grow mold or mildew.

It is possible to treat wooden containers with sealants to make them last longer; however, this must be done several times and will add to the amount of time required to care for the plant and its container.

Paper

Containers made out of recycled paper are versatile, as they are made in every color and texture. They are also among the most lightweight of all planting pots. Most paper containers, however, are not sturdy enough to last more than a few years and will likely deteriorate sooner if they are used outdoors.

Paper plant pots are another type of container that can be made from home. They can be made from scrap paper you recycle and press around a mold to form the shape of the plant pot. If you have an inner pot inside the paper, the inner pot should be one made from plastic or clay to keep the soil and water from staining the pot. The outside of the pot can be painted or glazed to make it more attractive and unique. It will also hold up better against moisture.

If you make your own paper plant containers, check the bottom regularly for mold and mildew. The drainage holes in the bottom of the inner container will allow water to drain out, which could cause mildew growth. A triple-potting system can solve this problem. To arrange a triple container, place a container with drainage holes into a slightly larger pot that does not have holes. Then, place both into the paper plant container.

Glass

Glass can be used to form beautiful containers that are also works of art. Some of the most attractive and artistic containers are ones made from glass or crystal. Colored glass used to house a flowering plant can be every bit as beautiful as the flowers that grow in it. Glass also catches the light and can take on a glowing appearance if the pot is placed correctly.

A downside to glass is that it is heavy. A large planting pot made from glass is impractical. Indoors, a large glass pot would be difficult to move. Outdoors, it could be shattered if it were knocked over in inclement weather. Gardeners with children also might feel a glass pot represents a danger to children who could knock it over or drop it on their feet.

Recycled and "art" planters

Container gardeners often have the most fun with containers that are art pieces or recycled items. These containers can be virtually anything that can hold soil or a smaller plant pot. An old shoe, a basket, a concrete block,

or an empty margarine tub are all items that can be used to start a container garden.

To find unexpected items to use as pots, conduct a few thrift store search missions. Anything with an opening at the top might potentially be recycled into a unique plant container.

An ornamental Medusa Pepper plant is being grown in an antique, cast-iron teapot.

Container Types

In addition to the material used to make the container, there are also a number of container types from which to choose. The type of container chosen should take into account the type of plant, size of the plant, and space available. Also consider which type of container is most convenient for you to take care of and which you will enjoy having around your home.

Hanging

Hanging pots are good for plants growing in trailing vines that need a good deal of space outside the container. Some fruit and vegetable plants, such as squash and strawberries, can be grown in hanging pots. Some of these might need a trellis or other support beside the hanging pot to allow the plant something to cling to for support.

Hanging containers are good space savers if you have little space for the plants or you want to fit as many plants as possible in a sunny spot. They are especially useful on porches and terraces. With a few hanging pots, the porch or terrace will still have room to accommodate smaller plant containers and the people who want to use the area.

Although hanging plants are attractive and it can be fun to watch the plants grow out of the pot and trail downward, they can be more complicated and time consuming to take care of. You will periodically have to take the plants down to check their soil, cut away dead leaves, and add fertilizer. If you find this physically difficult or an inconvenience you do not want, you might not want to choose hanging pots.

Window box

A window box is the ideal solution for a home that has little outdoor space and no porch or balcony. A window box can grow a number of compact plants in a small space and provide them with sunlight and rainfall.

A number of city residences have limited outdoor space, and the window box might be the only available outdoor area for growing. In those cases, make the best use of the window box by installing a large window box to grow a variety of plants. You should also look at the width of the plants you want to grow and choose plants that need little space around them. When growing plants in a window box, keep in mind the box will likely be shaded by the building during part or all of the day. Shade plants are usually grown best in window boxes.

Garden pots

Garden pots are generally the small, portable pots everyone is familiar with. These come in every size and shape but are generally round and tapered from top to bottom. Pots also come in self-watering varieties that have a reservoir of water in the base. These pots can make container gardening easier for gardeners who are short on time.

Oversized planters

Large container plants are usually grown in oversized planters. These can contain a tree or other large plant, or they might be used to grow many plants in a single container. A long row of plants that have runners — long vines that can grow their own roots — will expand sideways quickly. Plants such as squash and some strawberry varieties are perfect for oversized planters. A strawberry patch will grow well in an oversized planter that has plenty of room for its fast-growing runners.

Although they are often used outdoors for ornamental trees, citrus trees, and berry bushes, oversized planters can also be used indoors. If you want to grow a large number of smaller plants, such as miniature tomato plants, an oversized planter will keep them all in one container. An oversized planter makes it possible to grow large plants, but it can be difficult, or even impossible, to move when it is filled with soil.

Containers Come in all Sizes and Shapes

Planters come in all shapes and sizes, and for art student Steven Wheen, they even come in the form of potholes.

When Wheen was biking around London, he was disappointed by the large number of potholes and decided to apply his green thumb to the situation.

Wheen started "guerrilla gardening," or planting without permission on public land, using the potholes as his containers.

Many others have followed his lead, and guerrilla gardening has happened around the world since the 1970s. People have been turning to public lands for interesting and unusual containers for their plants.

Wheen even turned his pothole planting into a project and plans to include his blog, **http://thepotholegardener.com**, in his master's thesis, according to The Globe and Mail.

As GuerrillaGardening.org **(www.guerrillagardening.org)** reports, guerilla gardening has increased lately as people turn to their surroundings to beautify the city and share their love for gardening.

The Importance of Drainage

Every container must have a system of drainage. This is vital for the root system to keep it from sitting in too much moisture. No matter what size, shape, or type of container you have, it must provide for drainage.

Water is needed regularly by most plants, but like anything, too much of a good thing can be destructive. In the wild, plants have the surrounding soil to absorb water if too much is added to the soil. Outdoor plants also have the sunlight to rapidly evaporate the water in the soil.

In a container, these conditions must be replicated to keep too much water from accumulating in the soil. Every pot, no matter what the type or size, must have a few drainage holes in the bottom large enough to allow any excess water to drain out in a timely manner. If the holes are too small and allow only a few drops of water to drain, the drainage might not be fast enough to keep the water from damaging the plant and the soil.

Many decorative or recycled planters have no drainage holes. These are generally used as outer containers around smaller containers that do have adequate drainage holes to release excess moisture. Some gardeners add drainage holes to decorative pots with a drill or add drainage systems within their plant pots. This can be done by elevating the plant within the pot onto a block of foam.

Water is good for plants, right?

Every plant needs water to survive, but too much water will kill most plants. Unless the plant is a water or swamp plant, such as an azalea, too much water is one of the fastest killers among container plants. The right balance between too much and too little water must be struck to keep the plant at its healthiest.

A container that does not have adequate drainage can easily keep too much moisture in the soil. This will lead to root rot, which kills the plant quickly. Too much moisture in the soil can also lead to fungal infections and other plant diseases.

Salt buildup that accumulates on the surface of the soil is also a result of poor drainage. This buildup is unattractive to look at, but it is harmful to

the plant as well because it can burn the leaves of the plant. For plants with many low-lying leaves, this can mean a rapid death.

If you see white speckles along the top of the soil, the container might need more drainage. These speckles indicate a buildup of salt in the soil, which is indicative of too much water. If your container has no drainage holes, create holes in the bottom with a drill or a sharp instrument if possible. If the pot already has drainage holes, the problem might be that you are simply watering it too often and the soil is remaining moist for too long.

In some cases, excess moisture can rot the primary stem of the plant, killing it quickly. Watering the plant too often can cause the central stem to rot at its base. The entire plant can then break off, taking with it the entire above-ground portion of the plant.

To keep the plant from retaining too much water, add enough to allow a small amount to run out of the drainage holes in the bottom, which ensures the soil and container are draining properly. If you have a plant that is double-potted, remove the outer pot periodically to make sure the water has not pooled in the bottom of the container.

With too little water, the plant will not be able to pull nutrients out of the soil, and it will die from a lack of nutrition. How long this takes depends on the type of plant you are growing. Some plants can go weeks without showing any effects from a lack of water. Others, such as the peace lily, start wilting after less than a week.

An antique barrel cut in half also serves as a strawberry patch.

Chapter 4

TOOLS

I t is important to gather the right tools before you start your container garden. This will ensure that a gardening emergency can be solved before it gets out of control. These basic tools can be used for a wide variety of plants.

To save time and money while gardening, invest in a good, sturdy set of gardening tools and accessories. Although they will be more expensive up front, there will be no need to replace worn out or bent tools that do not hold up over time. You will not be stuck with broken tools as your plants outgrow their pots. High-quality gardening tools can be found in home improvement stores, gardening catalogs, and online gardening stores.

Gloves

Gloves might not be necessary in all cases. If you only want to grow a few small plants with smooth leaves and no thorns, you might not need them at all. However, if you plan to do a good deal of gardening, using gloves can keep your skin from becoming rougher due to the constant contact with the soil and the plants.

If you grow plants that have prickly leaves, as many vegetable plants do, using gloves is necessary. Tomato, squash, and cucumber plants are all extremely prickly and can actually leave splinters in your skin when you handle the stems and leaves.

If you are dealing with thick thorns or you spend plenty of time with plants that have prickly leaves, consider leather or thick vinyl gloves. Some of the higher-end gardening gloves have features such as neoprene — a tough, but flexible, material — in key areas to assist with dexterity. Some are made of goatskin or lambskin leathers. Silicone is used in some gloves to increase the durability and traction of the gloves.

Cloth gloves are inexpensive and are easy to find, but they have many disadvantages. They hold onto moisture and get heavy when wet. If the weather is cold, the moisture can lead to cold, numb hands. Cloth, even thick cloth, is no match for thorns or long-leaf prickles. If you are working with just a few small plants without thorns or prickly leaves and just want to keep your hands clean, cotton gloves might be enough to provide what you need.

Spray-on gloves are a new choice for gardeners. They are exactly what they sound like: gloves in a can. Hands are sprayed evenly with the silicon glove spray and then allowed to dry. When you are finished gardening, simply peel the gloves off and throw them away. These gloves offer some protection for the hands, but they are not as tough as leather gloves and will not prevent thick thorns or pointy branches from drawing blood.

If you are growing roses or thorny blackberry vines in containers, you will need something to protect your forearms as well as your hands to get into those bushes and vines and prune the appropriate areas. Consider buying a rose gauntlet, which is a long, elbow-length glove that provides thick, sturdy protection from thorns.

Trowel

A trowel is a tool that can be used for many different gardening tasks. This long, slender hand shovel can be used to mix your potting soil and fertilizer before your plant is planted. It can also be used to dig seed holes in the soil. Narrower trowels are useful for separating seedlings and digging out dead plants from among living ones. A wider trowel can be used like any other hand shovel, transplanting growing plants and digging out weeds that need to be removed.

It might take testing a few trowels to discover which ones you prefer for certain tasks. If you want to loosen outdoor plants to place them into containers, you might prefer a trowel with a serrated edge to cut through the topsoil or to cut away weeds. If you want to use it primarily for making seed and bulb holes, a serrated edge could make more of a mess than necessary.

Choose a thicker trowel to avoid bending it and rendering it useless. A trowel with thicker metal will be more expensive, but it will save time and hassle in the end.

Shovel

A full-sized shovel can be used for planting in larger planters that grow large plants and require large amounts of potting soil. The shovel can be used to fill the container with soil, add fertilizer, and transplant plants into and out of the container.

If you plan to eventually transplant your container plants into the ground, a shovel is necessary for breaking through the ground vegetation and mixing nutrients and fertilizer into the topsoil. You might also decide to dig up existing plants and transplant them into indoor containers during the winter. A shovel is needed to dig up the plants and provide enough soil around the roots to keep the roots from being damaged.

Like with a trowel, purchasing a high-quality shovel with thick metal is essential. A thinner metal might ruin the shovel the first time you use it on a patch of tightly compressed soil.

Shovels come in a number of varieties, but for many, the main features are the size and type of handle and whether the end is rounded or sharp. If you frequently need to cut through roots and vines or you have particularly difficult soil to cut through, a shovel with a pointed end will work best. If you have softer, looser soil, you might not need a pointed end. If you do not plan to transplant plants into and out of the ground, a rounded shovel is good for transporting soil from a potting soil bag into a planter. With a round-ended shovel, you will not have to worry about the shovel piercing the bag.

Clippers/Pruning Shears

Clippers of various sizes are needed for anyone who grows container plants. A small set of clippers can be used to cut away dead flowers and leaves cleanly. If you want to prune a plant that has thick stems, a pair of clippers or pruning shears is essential for making it through the stem in one cut to avoid damaging it. With shears that are too small or too dull, you may strip or crush the stem instead of making a clean cut.

Although a small pair of clippers is usually enough for pruning and cutting dead flowers away from small plants, larger plants, such as fruit trees and large bushes, can require a pair of pruning shears. Cutting back vines and thin branches is often necessary for cultivating the stronger branches and vines of a plant. Pruning shears are the ideal tool for the job, particularly when a plant is cut back for the winter to encourage new growth in the spring.

Watering Can

Watering cans are not necessarily essential, but they are convenient tools to have. If your plants are small, you might be able to water your plants with

a drinking glass, but refilling it many times to water all of the plants will add to the time it takes to care for your plants. A watering can be used for inside and outside plants, and it can be filled quickly. Using a watering can will take less time than refilling a smaller container many times, and it is more portable than using a garden hose.

Watering cans come in metal, plastic, and ceramic. The ceramic varieties are a little impractical, though they are pretty. Ceramic can crack, chip, and break — not the features you want in a tool that will get plenty of use and might be lugged onto balconies and roofs and into gardens.

Metal watering cans are the sturdiest type. Although older metal cans were infamous for rusting, today's metal watering cans are made to be functional, beautiful, and durable. Brass and copper are used in some of the higher-end watering cans. Some metal cans have long ends that make them useful for watering large window boxes or large container plants that need water in the soil and not on the leaves.

Plastic watering cans range from inexpensive, simply designed models to higher-end watering cans that have long spouts and some metal parts. Some of the most expensive plastic watering cans have plastic bodies and handles and metal spouts. Plastic watering cans stand up well against the elements and can be left outside without worry.

One watering can could be used for all of your watering tasks, or you can purchase specialty cans for different tasks. There are indoor and outdoor watering cans, with outdoors cans made to be sturdier than the indoor variety. Some gardeners prefer to keep a small, pretty watering can indoors and a larger, sturdier can outdoors for outdoor container watering.

Cultivating Fork

A cultivating fork looks like a trowel, but the end has pointed tines — the pointed ends of the tool — instead of a rounded edge. Some cultivating forks have tines that are straight while others have bent tines to allow the tool to provide more leverage. The bent designs resemble hoes that have a few tines on one end instead of a solid, flat end.

This tool can be useful for tilling small areas of soil or creating a depression in which to place seeds. If you have root-bound plants, a cultivating fork can be used to cut through the outer root growth to break up the bound roots. This helps the root ball to break up, to stretch out in the soil after being transplanted.

A cultivating fork might not be much help for planting in potting soil or taking plants out of a container to re-pot them, but it can be helpful if you dig up plants to put into containers or plan to replant container plants. A cultivating fork with a bent end can efficiently cut through ground foliage. The tines help the cultivating fork pull away the offending foliage or roots to make room for the transplant.

String or Garden Ties

Some plants need to have firm support while growing. This is especially important when the plant is grown in a container and cannot trail away to the nearest fence or tree. Some blueberry bushes, tomato plants, and other assorted plants need to be tied to a stake or other tall fixture as they grow.

Vines often need to be tied in order to grow in small spaces. Bean plants often need to be attached to stakes to keep them upright. Plants that trail out of a container and onto the ground not only take up more room, but they also risk more insect damage and fungal diseases from being exposed to the ground moisture for long periods.

Some gardeners use ordinary household string, pipe cleaners, twist ties, or yarn to hold plants in place. These have to be checked periodically and re-tied as the plant grows to allow the plant to grow without being pulled downward by the ties. There are also plant ties that are specially made to stretch with the plant as it grows so that it does not have to be changed as often.

Stakes or Trellises

A trellis can be a premade, wooden, bamboo, or plastic trellis available at any home improvement store, or build your own out of tall lumber or branches. A gazebo can also be used as a trellis for climbing plants.

Plants such as morning glories and bean plants grow upward quickly. Having a trellis in place before you plant them is important.

Stakes are needed for some smaller plants that cannot support themselves. If you want to grow orchids, stakes are necessary for holding up the long, narrow stems. Orchid growers can tie their orchid to a stake, but many prefer to use colorful plant clips to gently keep the stem in place against the stake.

Bamboo trellises are a good option for indoor container gardens because the weight of the bamboo is light and these trellises are attractive.

A tomato cage can be used for many plants — not just tomatoes. The cage can be set up around the plant inside a large container or around the

outside of a smaller one. The cage can be affixed to the ground if the container is outdoors on top of the soil. If the container is indoors, a more elaborate system will need to be used to anchor the cage down.

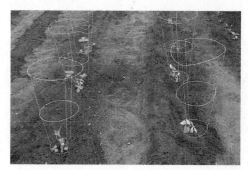

Full-size tomato plants, peppers, eggplants, blackberry vines, and bean plants need stakes or trellises to climb. Cucumber, squash, and watermelon plants often have long vines that can be hard to accommodate within a container. A trellis or tall stakes can help create a smaller area for the plant without stifling its growth.

If you supply a stake or trellis for a plant, put the seeds or seedling directly at the base of the support. This will enable the plant to grow directly upward onto the support without much early vine training to get the plant to climb. With a support directly above the plant, a plant with vines will begin climbing as soon as it is tall enough to do so.

If you need a stake for a flowering plant, use the shortest one possible. The stake should be slightly shorter than the full height of the mature plant. This will ensure the stake will not be readily seen when looking at the flowers.

CASE STUDY: A LOVE FOR GARDENING

Bethany Wieman
Bethanyw@gmail.com
www.soitgrows.com
Phone: (402) 933-5567

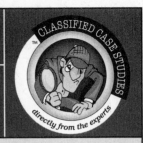

I have been growing container plants ever since I went off to college in 1993 and had to live in a dorm room. I think I was the only one in the dorm with a container full of herbs in the room. I could never convince my roommate to love my cinnamon basil, but I definitely enjoyed having the plants around.

I have grown almost every type of plant possible in containers — herbs, vegetables, succulents, small citrus trees, flowers, tomatoes, and even moss. My mom, a master gardener, instilled a love of gardening in me. When I run out of room in my raised beds for more plants, I do some container gardening instead. For apartment-dwellers and people who live in small spaces, container gardening might be the only option.

Container gardening also allows you to over-winter your favorite plants year after year. For example, I have a large rosemary plant that is about three years old now. It spends spring and summer outside, and I bring it in for the fall and winter. It is great to have fresh rosemary in the middle of winter and quite a psychological boost to have some of that greenery in the house.

Containers also allow you to add a pop of color to porches and patios. You can make your front door friendly and welcoming by flanking it with containers that spill over with colorful flowers. You can give your patio a tropical feel with containers of hibiscus or lantana. Containers give a house great curb appeal.

Another benefit of containers is they are very accessible; you do not have to kneel down on the ground to weed them, and they are less susceptible to soil-borne diseases.

People choose to grow food indoors because it is fun. Also, with the epidemic of childhood obesity and poor eating habits, it is especially important to get children involved in growing healthy food. Study after study has shown that children who are involved in growing fruits and vegetables are more likely to eat them.

It is also economical. If you go to the supermarket to buy fresh herbs, they are very expensive. Dried herbs lack flavor. If you have a few pots of your favorite herbs available, however, it is a breeze to clip some off and add them to your favorite dishes.

Gardening also gets in your blood. For those of us who are true gardening enthusiasts, it is hard to go through the winter months without seeing our favorite plants.

Adequate light can be a problem, especially if you are growing vegetables, herbs, or other plants that require a lot of light. Fortunately, this is easily remedied. Even a cheap fluorescent shop light will benefit plants. If you are working with houseplants, just read the tags. Most houseplants do quite well indoors with no supplemental lighting.

The number of plants generally manageable to house indoors depends on the square footage, natural light, and the size of the plants. Generally, if you are over-wintering outdoor plants, such as herbs and peppers, they will not grow very much at all during the winter, but you will have a head start on everyone else's plants once the growing season starts up again and you put them back outside. Some houseplants, such as ficus trees for example, will easily grow to the ceiling height of a room.

Succulents are great to grow in containers because they are typically slow growing. An aloe plant is always nice to have around because it is very soothing for burns; just snap off the tip of a leaf and rub it on the affected area.

Outdoors, peppers, tomatoes, herbs, flowers, and even the new columnar apple trees thrive in containers as long as they are large enough. Containers do not have to be fancy, either. You can even use a recycled five-gallon bucket with holes punched in the bottom for tomato plants, for example.

I have had very poor luck with roses in containers. Tomatoes will not do well if the container is not large enough. A tomato plant at peak production can drink between one to two gallons of water a day, so you need to have a container that can hold the plant, the water, and the soil. A lot of people put them in containers that are too small. Things like peonies, lilacs, clematis, and hostas are better left in the ground.

People are much more educated now about their food than they have been in the past. Farmers' markets have proliferated all over the country. Books such as *Fast Food Nation* and *The Omnivore's Dilemma* have really focused the public's attention on where food comes from. Then we have TV shows such as "Jamie Oliver's Food Revolution" that further publicize the American crisis of poor nutrition.

One of the advantages of growing your own food is being able to try different and unusual varieties. For example, Cherokee purple tomatoes are amazing, but they are hard to find in your typical grocery store. When I plant my own Cherokee purple plants, I have a steady supply of this delicious and unusual tomato.

Growing your own food is also incredibly convenient. In the spring, I enjoy heading out the back door and picking a salad for lunch.

If you are careful about separating your new plants from your existing collection for few days to make sure you are not bringing in any new pests, you can really minimize the trouble with that issue. Whiteflies are probably the most troublesome pests for indoor plants, but they can easily be avoided.

Insecticidal soap can handle most insects, and it is also safe for kids and pets. Some pests, such as the tomato hornworm for example, can easily be picked off an affected plant. Larger garden pests, such as rabbits, can be excluded from a garden area with fencing buried 6 to 8 inches into the soil.

Chapter 5

SOIL AND AMENDMENTS

W hen you garden in the soil outdoors, a great deal of factors can go wrong. Many soil types make it difficult to grow plants at all, and plenty of preparation is needed to ready some types of soil for growing healthy plants. In clay or dry soils, tilling and mixing are often needed to give the soil better drainage and aeration. Aeration is a loosening of the soil to allow water to drain through it. However, with container gardening, this tilling and mixing is not necessary.

Potting soil is a sterile soil type that is made to have good drainage and retain moisture at the same time. It is inexpensive and usually contains plenty of organic nutrients to allow plants to thrive without having to add much to the soil.

Choosing the Right Soil

Different plants require different things from the soil. Some plants, such as African violets, have specific soil requirements, which leads to the creation of specialized potting soil exclusively for those plants. In most cases, a standard potting soil will have a blend that can be used as-is or with the addition of a fertilizer to meet the needs of the specific plant.

To create a custom blend, many gardeners add components to the potting soil to make it conform better to the needs of their plants. Because peat moss absorbs so much water, it can be added to soil that will need to stay moist most of the time. Sand is sometimes added to give the soil a looser quality to allow more aeration. Fertilizers also can be added into the soil to give it the specific nutrients a plant needs.

Before you choose a commercial potting soil mix, take a close look at the label to make sure you know what you are buying. Without a careful look, you can end up with a poor-quality soil that will need plenty of preparation before it is ready to use.

Some potting soils are made up of one single organic material. Others come pre-mixed with several different materials. If the soil is labeled as potting soil or a container mix, it is a mixture of a few ingredients that together create a material that will hold onto moisture longer than most soil but will stay loose and allow plenty of air circulation and water drainage.

Potting mixes usually have a water-retaining material as well as a material that keeps the soil from becoming too compacted. Perhaps the most common moisture-retention materials are peat moss and ground tree bark. To keep the soil from clumping, vermiculite — a natural mineral — is often added to the mixture. Other non-clumping ingredients include pumice and perlite, two abrasive, natural substances. These materials are often present in these premade potting soils, but they can also be added in larger amounts if the plant requires it. If the soil you use clumps too much, consider adding extra perlite to the soil and mixing it well before adding it to the next container.

Some less-expensive potting soil brands use chunks of foam to keep the soil loose and provide aeration instead of sand or other organic components. Although this does work marginally well, the foam does not break down and is not environmentally friendly. If you want to use the potting soil outdoors or you often empty old plant containers onto the ground outside, the foam will stay on the ground and blow into the wind or stick to the grass after it rains. The resulting mess is unattractive and difficult to clean up.

Using a Quality Soil Blend

The bacteria present in outdoor soil is a part of a full ecosystem of insects, plants, and other environmental factors. That bacteria is kept in check in nature, but the same is not true for outdoor soil placed into a container. In this limited environment, the bacteria can grow out of control, which provides a poor environment for the plant you want to grow.

Outdoor soil also carries small insects and insect eggs and larvae that can later attack your plants and contaminate your other containers. The soil can contain a multitude of weed seeds that can sprout up quickly The soil outside has fungi spores that can lead to mold problems on your plants.

Nematodes, which are microscopic worms, are another serious concern when using outdoor soil. These worms might be tiny, but they are extremely plentiful. Each handful of outdoor soil contains nematodes by the thousand. These tiny worms are the most common multicellular creatures in the world, and they can feast on your plants, cause plant diseases, and invade your body. Roundworms, a type of nematode, are parasites that infect humans.

Although these are all natural problems that occur with outdoor gardening, one of the advantages of container gardening is these problems can be curbed or even eliminated altogether. Commercial potting soil is sterile and contains no nematodes, weed seeds, or harmful bacteria. It contains only ingredients that help plants to thrive.

Some gardeners choose to bake their outdoor soil to create sterile potting soil. Baking the soil will kill the bacteria and make the soil more suitable for container gardening, but it will not make the soil better at retaining moisture or add the organic materials that most plants need. In the end, the inexpensive price and easy availability of potting soil make it unnecessary to spend your days baking your outdoor soil in the oven.

Fertilizers

Fertilizers are put into the soil to add the nutrients specific plants need. They can be used to change the pH of the soil as well. The pH of the soil measures how acidic or alkaline it is. Some plants prefer acidic soil while others do better in less-acidic soil. Using the right fertilizer can result in faster growth, greener leaves, and abundant flowers, fruits, and vegetables. Plants absorb fertilizer through their roots once the fertilizer has been dissolved by the water in the soil. As it is dissolved, fertilizer is also washed away with frequent watering. Fertilizer is added to plants regularly to replenish this nutrient supply.

Each plant type has its own fertilizer timetable. Many plants do well when they are fertilized at the beginning of the growing season, in the early or late spring. Other plants need to be fertilized more often because of specific needs from the soil. Some of these finicky plants need to be fertilized every four to six weeks throughout the year. Still others need to be fertilized only during their blooming stage.

Fertilizers can be purchased as either fast-acting fertilizers or slow-release fertilizers. The fast-acting type can burn leaves and cause root damage to many plants. They can speed up the growth of plants, but they generally are not recommended for small gardens because of the possibility of leaf burn.

Slow-release fertilizer in granular form is generally recommended to prevent leaf and root damage.

Compost is a type of organic substance that offers plants an enormous boost of fertilizing nutrients. Some home gardeners create their own compost pile or use a compost tumbler to compost their food waste with their soil. This provides container gardeners with a great, inexpensive, and useful fertilizer safe to use in containers.

Nutrients in fertilizers

Fertilizers use three main soil components to create the right nutrient balance for container plants. The first is nitrogen, an essential part of soil. A lack of nitrogen in the soil can lead to stunted plant growth. In nature, nitrogen is supplied through animal manure and lightning, so using a fertilizer that contains this nutrient is certainly preferable for indoor plants over these alternatives.

The second component of fertilizers is phosphorus. This nutrient is important for flower growth and can be added as either ground bone or ground rock. These are added to high-phosphorus fertilizers to add the necessary nutrient.

The third ingredient in the mix is potassium. This nutrient helps to grow stronger roots and more vigorous plants overall. It is helpful in fruit growth and is needed just before fruit begins to develop.

Fertilizers are usually rated with the percentages of these three nutrients. The first number is the percentage of nitrogen. The second number is the percentage of phosphorus. The third is the percentage of potassium. Different blends are used for different types of plants depending on what the plant needs most from the soil.

When purchasing a fertilizer for a specific plant, find out what the best fertilizer mix for that plant will be. It might be 10-10-10, 15-10-15, or any variation of the three numbers. The specific nutrient requirements of each plant will determine the best number. General fertilizers, such as slow-release beads, might not have a number specified. These are fertilizers that have a mixture of many soil nutrients and can be applied to many types of plants.

Fertilizers also are made specifically for edible plants. They are made to fertilize a broad spectrum of fruit and vegetable plants with general nutrients. They are also made to be non-toxic so the edible plant is not contaminated with toxic materials.

Watering granules

Watering granules are tiny crystals that absorb water and keep it in the soil longer than if the water ran straight through the soil and out through the drainage holes. These granules gradually release the water, which keeps the soil moist, but does not release the water quickly enough to cause moisture damage to the plant's roots or stem. The granules hold water in a gel form, so the additional moisture being held in the soil keeps the water available without making the soil soggy.

Many plants that grow fruit and vegetables, such as cucumber, tomato, and strawberry plants, need water constantly to stay healthy and produce, but the moisture can cause fungi to grow. Using watering granules can help fruit and vegetable plants have access to moisture at all times without the risk of fungi. The plant's roots can seek out the moisture directly from the granules and get water whenever it is needed. This is not only a time-saver, but it also is important for anyone who travels often or who forgets to water container plants.

If the plant is already established in the container, the granules can be sprinkled into the potting soil at the top or mixed into the top 1 to 2 inches of soil. When the soil is watered, the granules will hold onto the moisture and will become heavier and eventually settle lower into the container. The granules can be added to a container by mixing them into the potting soil before putting the soil into the container.

CASE STUDY:
FROM THE PERSPECTIVE OF
A NEW CONTAINER GARDENER

Janis Bennett
Janis.bennett@yahoo.com
http://freelancewriterroad.com
Phone: (781) 447-3173

Other than houseplants, we have never grown anything in containers.

This year, my husband and I are growing a container garden for the first time. Usually, we have a small plot of dirt in our yard used for gardening. We decided to try container gardening so we can use the old garden area for a koi pond and sitting area.

The advantages of container gardening include an easy clean-up at the end of the season, the ability to grow food in an area that might not be feasible for a regular garden, and the ability to move the plants in and out of the sunlight as needed.

Also, it is a little simpler to make sure the plants receive the correct amount of water. It is easier to determine how much water is provided manually to a plant in a container than it is a plant outside in the ground.

People might choose to grow food indoors so they can grow all year around, thus reducing their grocery bill while promoting healthy eating. A person with physical restrictions might be able to take care of a container garden a lot easier than having to go outside to garden in the ground. People who live in apartments might like to grow food indoors because they typically do not have a yard in which to grow food.

The main problems with indoor container gardening are bugs might be more attracted to your plants and might find their way inside your home. Also, space can be an issue, and a person might not be able to grow every single type of fruit or vegetable her or she desires. Lastly, making sure the plants are in an appropriately sized container is important so they can grow and produce food. Plants will not grow large enough to produce food if they are in containers that are too small. Approximately ten plants make up a generally manageable indoor container garden.

In my experience, tomatoes do very well in large containers, and the bright red-colored fruit looks great with my home décor. The tomatoes must have some sort of support while growing, such as a stick or mesh, for the vines to attach to. Our lettuce is also doing well in containers, and rabbits are not able to reach it.

All the information available about organic food has really boosted the popularity of growing your own food. One of the advantages of growing your own food is you can grow all your favorites. You also have control on the types of treatments used on your plants, such as pesticides and chemicals. A gardener can decide and control exactly what goes onto the plants or into the plant soil.

A lot of money can be saved by growing your own food. When all your vegetables are grown at home, you can skip the entire produce section in the grocery store. Kids will be more apt to eat veggies they have watched grow or even helped care for, which will result in healthier children.

Chapter 6

START WITH SEEDS OR START WITH PLANTS?

Every gardener has his or her own preferences about how to start a new plant — with either a seedling or a handful of seeds. In some cases, the decision might amount only to personal preference. In others, it might come down to the time of year, the cost of the plants and seeds, and the ease of growing a plant from a seed.

Not all plants are easily grown from seeds and are instead divided or planted from cuttings to create new plants. A cutting is a small portion of a plant cut from the parent plant and used to propagate a new plant. A plant cutting has no roots and usually includes at least one leaf. African violets can be started with just a cutting. A single leaf can be a cutting or a stem containing one or more leaves.

Why Start with Seeds?

Seeds are invariably cheaper than buying seedlings. For the same price as a few young plants, a gardener can buy enough seeds to grow a field. The price alone tempts many gardeners into trying to grow many plants from seeds. Because a packet of seeds is inexpensive, gardeners can attempt to grow many plants at once.

Choosing to grow with seeds is also a way to continue growing the same plants you have grown and enjoyed before. Saving seeds from your fruits, vegetables, and flowers will allow you to grow the progeny, or offspring, of the plant you enjoyed.

If you have little space and want to grow plants indoors in containers before planting them in the ground, growing seeds is a good way to grow a large number of plants without taking up much room. Seed trays can house 50 or more young seedlings in just the space of a small tabletop. Having that many larger plants indoors can be difficult even if a large space is available.

Plants that do not transplant well need to be sown and grown in the same space. Plants such as carrots tend to be fast-growing and need to have the seeds started in one pot and the plant left largely undisturbed until harvest time.

Why Start with Plants?

Some plants simply do not grow well from seeds. Others are propagated from seeds, but the process of getting the seeds to germinate and the seedlings to grow into smaller plants is extremely complicated and can take months. Gerbera daisies, for instance, grow well from seedlings and are hardy as long as they have water and sunlight. However, they are very difficult to grow from seed. Most Gerbera daisy seeds will not sprout, and the germinated seeds might not grow very large. Germination is the plant's process of emerging from its seed and beginning its growth.

Another upside to starting a container garden with plants instead of seeds is the instant gratification factor. Growing from seeds can be a lengthy, boring task. If you are teaching children how to garden, they might lose interest long before the seeds germinate. With plants, you get to see the plants from day one instead of waiting weeks or even months.

Seeds

Starting a fruit, vegetable, plant, or herb garden from seeds can be difficult and time consuming. However, there are several distinct advantages to using them. Among these is the availability of even the most exotic seeds.

Seeds can sometimes be so large that just one or two will fit into a seed pot. They can also be so small that they are difficult to see with the naked eye. Some seeds are so tiny that growers add powder to the seeds to carry the seeds and make it easier to spread them across the soil.

Buying seeds

When you begin to look for seeds sold at stores, you will start to notice how pervasive they are. They are sold in most mass merchandise, hardware, home improvement, and gardening stores. Many grocery stores and drug stores also sell them. In addition, many seed catalogs are available to order by mail. Online seed stores often specialize in certain types of seeds, such as roses or exotic plants, while others sell hundreds of different plant seeds.

Unless you buy very exotic, rare seeds, most seed packets are extremely inexpensive. Less than $5 can generally purchase several seed packets, even if the seeds are bought online or through a catalog and must be shipped to you.

Heirloom seeds

Heirloom seeds are from plant lines that are not hybridized with other lines. The plants are open-pollinated and are not cultivated for any new traits. Open pollination is the natural pollination that occurs when pollen is spread by wind, bees, or birds. They are not genetically modified and have not been selectively bred by produce companies.

Many heirloom lines have been in use for centuries. Plants such as tomatoes that change little over time have extremely long heirloom lines. Some of the heirloom tomato seeds on the market grow tomatoes the same size, shape, color, and taste that people ate more than 400 years ago.

Many people prefer to buy heirloom seeds because the fruit and vegetables resulting from those seeds are different from the few varieties available in grocery stores. They are novelty items that expand the smells and flavors most people are accustomed to.

Open-pollinated heirloom seeds were cultivated over centuries by people who wanted better, hardier plants that yielded plenty of fruit and vegetables. They are generally more durable than hybrid plants and adapt better to new ecosystems. Some gardeners say the flavors of heirloom lines are better than the modern hybrids'.

Hybrid seeds

Hybrid seeds are seeds from plants that have been crossed from two different parental lines. The seeds are the first generation results from the crossing of the two lines. Many hybrid seeds are sterile. Others have unpredictable outcomes in the resulting plant and the edibles it produces. The new plants might end up looking and tasting like one of the parent lines or like a combination of both.

Hybrid seeds often need more care than open-pollinated seeds. They are often bred to produce the highest possible yield without any emphasis on hardiness or other important traits. With hybrid seeds, disease and pests can be a major problem in the resulting plants.

If your only intent is to have the highest yield possible, you might choose to plant hybrid seeds. However, the seeds from the resulting plants usually cannot be saved to grow the next generation of plants.

How seeds work

Seeds are created by a plant's sexual reproduction. They are the embryos of the plants they came from. These embryos come with a little bit of food inside the covering in which they are packaged. The embryo consumes the food within the seed covering until it is able to leave the seed covering to seek out additional food.

The seed coat exists to protect the embryo from insects, plant diseases, and too much moisture. Germination is the process of becoming ready to sprout. The right conditions must be present to make germination happen, and germination can take weeks for some plants. When the seeds are ready to germinate, the seeds begin to grow actively. To make this happen, some water must be absorbed through the seed coat. There must also be the right level of light, the right temperature, and the right amount of oxygen around the seed.

The first part of the seed to emerge from the seed coat is the radicle. This will grow into the plant's main root. The embryo's hypocotyl is the part that grows into the plant's stem. These parts continue to grow and strengthen, making the embryo into a seedling.

How to plant seeds

Every seed has its own requirements that bring about the germination of the seed. Many seeds need sunlight to germinate. Those seeds are surface sown to allow sunlight to reach the seeds. Many flower seeds require only a one-fourth-of-an-inch covering of soil or less, which allows sunlight to filter down through the soil to the seeds.

Most seeds also require moisture to germinate. Although some begin sprouting after a week of moist soil and sunlight, others need months of cold weather and/or moisture to sprout.

The most important thing to do when planting seeds is to follow the directions for each individual seed type; just because one plant grew well when surface sown does not mean that the next one will. This book will provide basic growing instructions for a variety of plants. When growing specialized plants or plants not included in this book, you should consult the directions on the seed packet.

Starting seeds indoors

Seeds can be started indoors in a number of different containers. Seed pots are tiny pots, usually 1 to 2 inches across, for an individual seed to germinate and become a seedling. They are plastic, terra cotta, and cardboard. The cardboard variety is meant for planting directly into the ground or into a larger pot when the seedling is too large for the pot because the cardboard will decompose. These are often the easiest pots to use for seedlings that will have to be transplanted promptly.

Seed trays are another platform for starting seeds and growing seedlings. The trays are shallow flats with small indentations for the individual seeds. These are used to grow a large number of seedlings before transplanting them into larger individual containers.

Perhaps a simpler version is to start seeds in a large container and thin out the seedlings to allow the strongest seedlings to grow into larger plants. This means not transplanting fragile young seedlings. If the plants are small, it might mean not having to transplant the seeds at all.

Transplanting your seedlings

When transplanting seeds from cardboard pots or seed pots made from peat moss, cut the bottom off the pot and break apart the pot to make it easier for the roots to escape, and then plant the pot directly into the soil. The pot will eventually biodegrade into the soil. For terra-cotta seed pots, use a trowel to dig out the seedlings or simply turn the pots upside down and tap the pot to get the plants loose. If the seedlings are in seed trays, they can be gently lifted either by hand or with a trowel and placed into their new, larger pots.

The new pot should have a bit of potting soil in the bottom before you start the transplant. Then, hold the seedling in the pot so the stem and leaves are above the outer rim of the container. Fill in the rest of the container with potting soil around the seedling's roots.

The soil around the roots should be packed tight enough to allow the plant to stand upright, but packing it too tightly can damage the plant. It can restrict the roots' growth and impede the flow of oxygen through the soil.

Plants

When you choose to start your container garden with plants, it is important to know exactly what you are buying. Buying the wrong plants can result in plants that do not survive, contaminate your garden, or make your gardening project more difficult than it needs to be.

Choosing plants

If you buy seedlings or more mature plants, it is important to inspect them carefully to ensure the plants are healthy and are not carrying pests or diseases back

to your garden. The following are several telltale signs that problems exist in the plant and that it is not healthy:

- Wilted or yellowing leaves indicate health problems. Slight wilting might only mean the plant needs to be watered and is currently under water stress. Yellowing leaves can mean insect damage, plant disease, or poor soil quality. Other color problems such as white, black, or brown speckles can mean insect or disease damage.

- Leaves that have holes, pieces missing from the tips, or obvious areas that have been chewed likely have insect damage. A spindly and thin plant with little foliage may have had too little light during its most critical development. Woody plants with damaged stems and branches may have damage 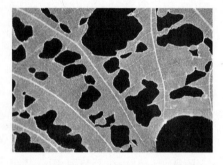 that will leave them vulnerable to attack by insects and fungi.

- If possible, also look at the roots to make sure they are in good condition. Although it is common to have nursery plants display some root-bound growth, extreme root bind may spell an inability of the plant to recover. If you cannot see any soil through the circular growth of the roots, the plant is not a good bet. If the roots look and feel dry, the plant likely is not destined to live long. Even a quick watering may not be enough to save a plant in this condition.

- If weeds are growing in the pot, avoid purchasing it. There could be many weed seeds in the soil, and those weeds will be transplanted into your container garden. Once weeds have been introduced, they can be quite difficult to eradicate.

Buying plants

When it comes to buying plants, there are many options. Local nurseries grow and sell plants, and large-scale garden stores sell plants by the thousands. Some plants, such as herbs, are sold in grocery and drug stores. Mass merchandise stores also have a firm footing in the plant market. Plants at these stores are sold in peat, cardboard, plastic, and sometimes terra-cotta pots.

Local growers who sell directly to the public can be a valuable resource for buying plants. To find out whether there are local growers who sell directly, check out the local farmer's market or ask someone in your local nursery.

A young plant can be bought for anything from $2 to $20 depending on the plant type. For most fruit and vegetable plants, seedlings in small plastic or peat pots usually cost less than $5. The larger the plant, the more these plants will cost. The cost of flowering plants usually depends on how common the plant is. An exotic plant that is hard to grow will cost more than one that flourishes freely and needs little care. Flowers such as pansies, chrysanthemums, and other common flowering plants cost little unless the plant itself is large. Flowering plants are usually sold in plastic containers to allow re-potting elsewhere or in ceramic, concrete, wood, or terra-cotta containers meant to house the plants until they outgrow that container.

Re-potting your purchased plants

When your newly purchased plants are home, it is important to start taking care of them right away. Do not allow the plants to sit in the store pot for long. The plant will likely be root bound and might need to be fertilized. Re-pot the plants as soon as possible.

Water the plants as soon as you get home to ready them for transplanting. Then, check for any bound roots. If you lift the plant from the container and see roots covering the soil in a circular pattern, the plant is root bound. This condition results from a plant being in a pot that is too small. Bound roots should be cut away with scissors before the plant is re-potted. Fill the new pot with enough potting soil to bring the plant up above the soil line and place the plant into the pot. Then, fill in the sides with more potting soil.

Companion Planting

Companion planting is the process of planting two or more plants together that can help the other in some way. A plant can provide pest control or some other benefit to the other plant that enables the two to withstand the normal assaults they face. Sometimes, companion planting is a way to provide nutrients to the soil from one plant to the other. This reciprocal relationship can mean less maintenance to the plants because fertilizer will not need to be applied.

Some plants have natural defenses that can defend not only themselves but the plants around them as well. A plant with thorns can help protect a plant intertwined with it from animal predators. Other plants have smells that create a protective barrier by attracting good insects or repelling harmful insects or wild animals.

African marigolds are plants that repel insects by releasing a chemical toxic to certain insects, such as beetles and nematodes. Planting one or two other plants in a container with this plant can mean pest resistance for all of the plants in the container. For example, an African marigold might be planted with an herb that is susceptible to pests to keep the pests away.

Companion planting can also be useful when one plant needs shade or dappled light. Growing a tall plant that needs direct sunlight with a shorter plant that needs shade is a beneficial arrangement for both plants. In outdoor containers, the use of larger plants to shield smaller plants from wind and cold is called nurse cropping.

CASE STUDY:
STRAIGHT FROM THE EXPERT

Kerry Michaels
About.com's Guide to
Container Gardening
containergardening.guide@about.com
www.containergardening.about.com
Phone: (207) 233-8555

I have been growing container plants for the past ten years. I have been the guide to container gardening for About.com for more than two years.

The advantages of container gardening are *huge*, especially if you hate weeding. It is a way to garden in places that are impossible to garden traditionally. It allows you to garden 30 stories up in a skyscraper or in the middle of an asphalt parking lot. Container gardening is also a way to garden that is less overwhelming than traditional gardening.

Growing food indoors is difficult, but growing herbs is easy and incredibly satisfying if you have enough light or can use grow lights. There is really nothing better than fresh herbs to turn a mundane dish into something spectacular. Growing herbs is less expensive and can be more convenient than buying them.

Indoor container gardening is all about choosing the right plants for the conditions you have — that and watering them properly.

The number of plants that can generally be managed indoors completely depends on your space and ability to care for your plants. For indoor air quality, experts recommend one plant for every 100 square feet. The list of the best plants to grow in containers is huge. You really can grow almost any plant in a container.

Studies have shown people are interested in growing their own food because they like the taste and feel it is a healthier and less expensive alternative. They also like it because it is really a fantastically satisfying experience to eat something you grow.

Some advantages to growing your own food are knowing the food has not been treated with unknown pesticides and it does not have E. coli. It is also cheaper, it tastes better, and it teaches children where food comes from.

There are all sorts of bugs and blights that can affect any plant — indoors or out. The biggest problem is usually people either over-water or under-water their plants.

To get rid of pests without using pesticides, the first step I take is to wash the plant. If it's outside, I hose it down and make sure I get the underside of the leaves. Next, I move on to using an insecticidal soap.

Chapter 7

GROWING HERBS IN CONTAINERS

Herbs have as many uses as they do varieties, and they are hardy plants to grow. Many people who enjoy cooking start growing their own herb gardens to have fresh ingredients on hand, but there are many other reasons to grow them. Many herb plants give off a pleasant odor from their leaves. Even if they do not have flowers, they can add a pleasant aroma to the room. Lemon verbena, rosemary, and mint plants are well-known for their pleasant smell as well as for their uses as edible plants.

Food Use

Many herbs have strong flavors and require just a pinch to flavor a family meal. A little bit of rosemary or sage can greatly change the flavor of a dish, and both are compact and easy to grow. Herbs also add nice aromas to dishes. Even plain white rice can be given a different flavor and smell with the addition of a pinch of herbs.

Many herb plants have flavorful leaves, which makes it easy to harvest a little of the plant to flavor a dish. Instead of needing a root component or a fruit that grows for a short time, simply cutting off a leaf and adding it to your recipe will give the dish an entirely new flavor.

Medicinal Use

Herbs have been used for their medicinal qualities since before recorded history. They are used to aid in digestion, clear up the skin, and treat mild depression. Lemon verbena is a fragrant herb used for centuries to treat stomach ailments.

Mint is used to treat toothaches, smooth skin, and aid with digestion. It also has anti-nausea properties. Feverfew is taken to treat fevers or migraines. Witch hazel has been used since the Middle Ages to clarify the skin and heal blemishes. St. John's wort has been medically proven to help relieve depression. Aloe is known to help with skin irritation and burns.

Growing these herbs in your home is a way to have these plant medicines around anytime they are needed. For people who try to live a natural lifestyle, the plants can be the equivalent to a medicine chest.

Bath and Beauty Use

Varieties of herbs are used in bath and beauty products, often for the soothing smell of the herb. The smell of lavender is known to calm the nerves. Lavender is used in bath products, soaps, shampoos, and bath gels to release the calming smell.

Calendula is used in bath treatments and lotions because of its skin-soothing properties. It is also used in shampoos to give your hair a pleasant scent. Rosemary is used for its astringent properties to tighten the pores of the face. Chamomile is soothing to the skin and leaves beauty products with a light fragrance.

Some people enjoy making their own bath and beauty products at home using their own garden-grown herbs. Some people choose to use the flowers or leaves directly without mixing them into a preparation. Throwing a few dried lavender flowers into the bathtub can give the bath a soothing smell, for example.

Home Cleaning and Décor Use

Herbs can be used to spruce up a home in many ways, from cleaning to decorating with dried specimens. Herbs are used in homemade recipes for cleaning carpets and mattresses. Sachets of fragrant herbs are kept in drawers and laundry rooms to freshen the smell of laundry and linens.

Herbal potpourri made from dried herbs can retain their smell for years. Some herbs, such as lavender, can be used to keep moths away from clothing and add a fresh scent.

Dried herbs also can be used as wall décor, in dried flower arrangements, and as additions to scrapbooks. The live plants are also used for aesthetic purposes. A tiny mint plant tucked onto a shelf adds a little color and life to a room.

Growing herbs in containers is, in itself, a type of home décor. Many herbs are attractive plants in their own right and often bloom with small, beautiful flowers. Growing herbs in small pots around the home is a way of decorating with living plants that also smell good and clean the air.

Herbs are Easy to Grow in Containers

Herbs generally need little care and grow well in small containers. They do need light throughout the year. A lack of winter sunlight can stunt the growth of the plants. Herbs should be inspected for pests regularly and watered often. The soil and container should allow for good drainage. Most herbs require significant sunlight each day. If your herb containers are indoors, choose a window that has Southern exposure to ensure as much sunlight as possible. West-facing windows are a good second choice.

Before fertilizing an herb plant, check the following section for the proper fertilization schedule and type. With some herbs, over-fertilizing will have a negative effect on the taste of the plant. Most herbs need only seasonal fertilization to keep them healthy. Each listed herb will contain information about fertilization times and types.

You can start your herbs in a seed flat. A flat is simply a long tray that has a number of small compartments that can accommodate seeds and a small amount of soil. Each compartment can be used to start several seedlings. When the seedlings sprout, choose one or two of the largest, healthiest seedlings and transplant these seedlings into a larger pot.

When growing herbs in containers, keep a number of small plant pots on hand for transplanting. Most herbs are small enough to grow in a pot that is 12 inches or fewer in diameter. Keeping several 6- and 12-inch pots on hand will allow you to transplant a number of different seedlings into pots and accommodate the growth of the larger varieties.

In addition to containers, keep potting soil and peat moss on hand. Both will be needed regularly for fertilization and transplanting. A general commercial potting soil will work for growing virtually any herb. Keep a bag of sterile sand available as well for herbs that prefer sandy soils. The sand can be mixed with the potting soil to create the ideal soil condition.

A Complete List of Container-grown Herbs

Each herb variety has its own light, temperature, and sun needs. Even within one plant species, there can be many varieties that have slightly different needs. The following sections provide guidelines for growing the major herb types.

Basil

Botanical name: *Ocimum basilicum*

Common name: Basil

Family name: *Lamiaceae*

Origin: Asia

Light: Full sun

Size and growth: 12-24" in height

Minimum temperature: 50° Fahrenheit

Blooming season: Summer

Outside hardiness zone: 4-9

Best time to prune: Spring

Common pests or diseases: Aphids

Fertilizer: Fish emulsion

Unique characteristics/growing tips: One frost will kill the plant if left outdoors overnight.

Description:

Basil is a versatile herb used in a number of recipes to add flavor. An aromatic plant, it can also be use as a garnish to dress up a plate of food. Basil needs plenty of sunlight and will not grow well in cold temperatures. In general, daytime temperatures should be in the 70s if the plant will be kept outdoors. Keep your container in the windowsill or outdoors for full sunlight. If the leaves turn pale, the plant needs more sunlight.

Basil can be started from seeds, or you can buy a seedling at most grocery stores and nurseries. With seeds, far more varieties are available than are usually sold in plant or grocery stores. When planting from seeds, it takes approximately three months for the plant to reach its full height. Seeds and seedlings will grow with regular potting soil, though some gardeners add a little sterile sand into the mix to allow for better drainage. Add fertilizer with a high nitrogen count once during the summer. Fish emulsion is often used as a fertilizer to promote leaf growth.

Basil is susceptible to over-watering. Allow the soil to dry out briefly before watering it again. Be prepared to re-pot it every few months to accommodate growth. The largest pot needed is a 12-inch pot. Once the plant is approximately 6 inches tall, start pruning the top of the plant to keep it from getting too tall and thin, known in growing circles as being "leggy." A leggy plant develops long, thin stems instead of a shorter, lusher plant. Pruning also slows down the plant's growing timeline, which means it will take longer to produce seeds. Once seed production is underway, the leaves will lose their strong flavor.

The hardiness of basil and its small size make it an ideal herb to grow in a container. Dwarf basil varieties are the perfect size for indoor growing, and they grow numerous leaves that are good to use while cooking. You can cut off the leaves at any time during the plant's life. The leaves are said to be tastier when the plant is young, but be sure to leave enough leaves on the plant to keep it alive. The plant needs to keep at least four or five large leaves to stay healthy.

Borage

Botanical name: *Borago officinalis*

Common name: Borage, ox-tongue

Family name: *Boraginaceae*

Origin: Mediterranean

Light: Full sun to partial shade

Size and growth: 18-36" in height

Minimum temperature: 60° Fahrenheit

Blooming season: April-July

Outside hardiness zone: 7-10

Best time to prune: Whenever growth needs to be controlled

Common pests or diseases: None

Fertilizer: High phosphorus fertilizers

Unique characteristics/growing tips: Borage is notorious for attracting bees due to its bright blue flowers.

Description:

Borage is a large herb plant that has edible leaves and edible flowers. The blue, star-shaped flowers are pretty on salads and can even be made into candies. The young leaves also can be used in salads. The leaves taste and smell like cucumbers. Eating borage is said to be good for fevers and constipation. The leaves can also be used in potpourri because of their fragrant smell. Though borage is edible, it is grown as an ornamental herb by some gardeners. The gray-green leaves and multitude of flowers make it an attractive part of a container garden.

Borage is an annual. It grows quickly and has a tendency to take over other plants easily. It should not be planted in the same container with other plants. Use regular potting soil, and do not fertilize unless growth stops. If you need to fertilize because of slow growth, use a fertilizer with high phosphorus. Keep the plant in direct sunlight.

Borage plants are hardy and have few pest or disease problems. They grow best when grown from seed, and they do grow very quickly. Often, the biggest problem is keeping the growth in check to keep the plant's size more manageable. Cutting off new leaves when the plant is growing can help keep its branches shorter and the plant more compact.

Borage has traditionally been known as bee plant and bee bread because of its tendency to attract bees from miles around. If you are allergic to bees, planting borage is not a good idea unless it is kept inside and away from open doorways. It should generally be kept away from play areas outdoors and common areas where people with bee allergies might spend time.

Chamomile

Botanical name: *Matricaria recutita*

Common name: German chamomile, Roman chamomile

Family name: *Asteraceae*

Origin: North Africa, Europe, and Asia

Light: Partial shade to full sun

Size and growth: 9-24" in height

Minimum temperature: 55° Fahrenheit

Blooming season: Late spring-summer

Outside hardiness zone: 4-7

Best time to prune: Prune away dead leaves in the fall

Common pests or diseases: Aphids

Fertilizer: Gentle, slow-release fertilizer

Unique characteristics/growing tips: The floral fragrance can repel pests.

Description:

Chamomile can be an annual or a perennial depending on the type you choose. The perennial variety, Roman chamomile, grows to approximately 9 inches tall. The annual, German chamomile, grows to approximately 24 inches. The annuals will re-seed themselves if you allow the seeds to fall into the soil. To help the plant re-seed, do not mulch the soil.

Chamomile is known for its calming effect when used in teas and bath water. It is also used in shampoos and lotions. Some gardeners grow it just for the fragrant smell of the plant. The light scent of chamomile makes it perfect for potpourri and sachets or to keep in the home to lighten the smell. It is often planted near cucumber plants because the smell of the chamomile plant wards off bugs.

Young chamomile plants need limited sun, but established plants thrive in full sunlight. The plants need plenty of water, so do not allow the soil to be dry for long. Chamomile is a hardy plant once it is established, but it is susceptible to aphids, tiny, destructive insects sometimes called plant lice. Aphids feed on the sap of plants and can sicken or kill plants by sucking the plant's nutrients through its stalks. Inspect it regularly by looking for tiny white dots along the stems and on the leaves.

Other than aphids and the occasional mealybug, a larger, equally destructive insect that lives in humid climates, chamomile has few pest or disease problems. It grows quickly and tolerates a wide variety of soil types. Medicinally, it is used to treat anxiety, sleeplessness, toothaches, and stomachaches and boost the immune system.

Chamomile does not need to be fertilized often. It is hardy and invasive because it began as a wildflower. It is tolerant of dry soil, but it will grow better if watered a few times a week. If growth slows, use a gentle organic fertilizer or compost to boost growth. Because of its invasiveness, do not plant chamomile in the same container as other plants.

If you start the plant from seeds, surface sow them. Leave the seeds uncovered by soil because the seeds need sunlight to germinate. Germination takes approximately one to two weeks.

Chives

Botanical name: *Allium schoenoprasum*

Common name: Chives

Family name: *Alliaceae*

Origin: North America, Europe, and Asia

Light: Full sun

Size and growth: 12-18" in height

Minimum temperature: 60° Fahrenheit

Blooming season: Summer

Outside hardiness zone: 3-9

Best time to prune: No pruning needed

Common pests or diseases: None

Fertilizer: General commercial fertilizer

Unique characteristics/growing tips: This plant will repel deer by giving off a scent the animals find offensive.

Description:

Chives are a common cooking herb that grows to approximately 18 inches in height. They are an herbal member of the onion family that have a milder taste than most onions. They are compact and only need approximately 6 inches of soil to grow well. They will tolerate most soil conditions but prefer to be watered often. They have almost no problems with disease or pests. They need little fertilizer, but a general fertilizer made for edible plants can help speed growth.

Although the green shoots and leaves of the chive plant are usually eaten, the flowers are also edible. The flowers taste like onions, and they can be used in salads or as a plate garnish. If you are growing your container garden outdoors and want to keep deer away, planting a border of chives around the garden is said to help.

Chives are perennial plants that can be planted with either seeds or bulbs. Because chives propagate themselves under ground with bulbs, new plants can be started by digging out the new bulbs in the spring or fall and planting them in new pots.

To separate new bulbs, dig up the plants and separate the bulbs by hand. Then, replant each bulb in its own container. The top of each bulb should be even with the surface of the soil. Adding a small amount of compost or bone meal to the potting soil can give the bulbs a good start.

Chives are easy-going plants that are not picky about their soil. They appreciate compost and other organic materials added to their soil, but they will tolerate almost any soil type. As long as chives are given proper lighting conditions and are watered once a week or so, they will thrive. The soil can be allowed to dry out in between waterings.

Indoors, chives will grow under fluorescent lamps placed about 2 to 4 inches above the plants. They will grow better under plant-growing lights, which are placed about 2 to 4 feet away from the plants. Outdoors, they prefer full sunlight but will tolerate partial shade.

To grow chives from seeds, start the seeds in March or April and keep the potting soil moist during germination. The seeds take about seven to ten days to sprout. When they are about a month old, they can be transferred to a larger pot and kept indoors or outdoors. If you are planting more than one chive plant in a container, keep about 8 inches between each plant.

Cilantro

Botanical name: *Coriandrum sativum*

Common name: Cilantro, coriander

Family name: *Apiaceae*

Origin: The Western Mediterranean and Southern Europe

Light : Full to partial sun

Size and growth: 2-3' in height, about 1 foot in width

Minimum temperature: 50° Fahrenheit

Blooming season: Summer

Outside hardiness zone: 3-11

Best time to prune: Late summer

Pests or diseases to watch for: None

Fertilizer: Organic, low nitrogen

Unique characteristics/growing tips: This plant's large taproot needs a tall potting space.

Description:

This annual is a remarkably hardy herb. It is not generally bothered by any pests and is not in danger of any plant diseases. When you grow cilantro, you are actually growing two cooking herbs — cilantro and coriander. The leaves of the *Coriandrum sativum* plant are what cooks call cilantro. When the plant goes to seed at the end of its growing cycle, those seeds are harvested as coriander.

Cilantro has a tall, thick taproot that is meant to anchor it to the ground, which keeps the plant in place even if drought makes the plant dry up or blows away the topsoil. A taproot is a thick, vertical root that forms the support for the other roots. The rest of the roots sprout directly from the taproot. Because of its large taproot, cilantro must be planted in a taller pot than would normally be needed for a plant of similar size. And, because the height and top diameter of planters are generally the same, this requires using a wide pot that might take up more room than your other herbs.

A container cilantro can be kept outside as long as the weather is above frost temperatures. Generally, the nighttime temperature should be 50 degrees Fahrenheit or higher if the plant is to be kept outdoors. Cilantro will grow best in full sun, but it will also tolerate partial shade.

If possible, avoid transplanting cilantro once the taproot forms. If you grow a cilantro seedling in a seed pot, it should be transplanted in a large container capable of holding the adult plant before the seedling is a month old. However, the best method of growing cilantro is to plant into the larger, adult-sized pot directly instead of using a seed pot and having to transplant the herb.

Cilantro is not fussy about its soil. It does not require any special fertilizer, though a low-nitrogen, organic fertilizer can be used. A high-nitrogen fertilizer can rob the leaves of their distinctive flavor, which is similar to parsley.

Dill

Botanical name: *Anethum graveolens*
Common name: Dill
Family name: *Apiaceae*
Origin: Eastern Europe
Light: Full sun
Size and growth: Up to 5' in height
Minimum temperature: 25° Fahrenheit
Blooming season: Summer
Outside hardiness zone: 3-11
Best time to prune: As needed

Pests or diseases to watch for: Caterpillars, mildew

Fertilizer: Compost, manure

Unique characteristics/growing tips: Avoid replanting because of deep taproot.

Description:

Like cilantro, both the leaves and the seeds of the dill plant are used in cooking. The foliage of the plant is called dill weed and is used in sauces, omelets, and vegetable dishes. The leaves are also used as a plate garnish. The seeds of the dill plant are generally what are called dill. The seeds are used in soups, salad dressings, breads, and other dishes.

Also, like cilantro, dill grows a long taproot that does not like being transplanted. Planting dill seeds or seedlings in a full-size pot large enough to house the adult plant is the best way to ensure the plant is not damaged or its growth stunted.

There are several varieties of dill, including dwarf varieties. The larger varieties reach 5 feet in height. The large taproots and root balls of these plants make them a poor choice for most containers. A large dill variety could be contained in a large outdoor planter, but its size would make it difficult to grow indoors.

Fernleaf is a dwarf variety of dill that is a better size for containers, because it reaches 12 to 18 inches in height. These plants produce small leaves and are often called baby dill. Dukat is a medium-sized dill that reaches 3 feet in height. Dukat is often used for its aromatic, flavorful seeds.

Caterpillars are a problem for dill plants grown outside. Cut away any damaged or dead leaves and stems to discourage caterpillars. The leaves are also susceptible to mildew if the plants are watered from the top. The watering should be done at the soil level to avoid leaving water on the leaves.

Dill has been used to pickle cucumbers for at least 400 years. It is a digestive aid and is used to make cucumbers tasty and easier to digest.

To use dill leaves, pick young leaves and use them within two days. After that time, the leaves wilt. To prolong the use of dill leaves, freeze them as soon as they are picked. Picking the young leaves delays the flowering of the plants. To collect dill seeds, wait for the flowerheads to turn brown. Then, cut the entire flowerhead from the plant and hang it upside down over a flat surface. The seeds will drop as the flowerhead dries. To ensure the dill plant will self-sow its seeds and return the next year, allow the flowerheads to remain in place. To harvest dill foliage, simply use scissors to cut away the portion you need.

Fennel

Botanical name : *Foeniculum vulgare*

Common name: Fennel

Family name: *Apiaceae*

Origin: The Mediterranean

Light: Full sun

Size and growth: Up to 2' in height, up to 1' in width

Minimum temperature: 50° Fahrenheit

Blooming season: Summer/fall

Outside hardiness zone: 4-9

Best time to prune: As needed

Pests or diseases to watch for: Aphids, white flies, caterpillars, root rot

Fertilizer: Fish emulsion

Unique characteristics/growing tips: The bulbs of this herb are edible and drought resistant. The large taproot makes transplanting difficult.

Description:

Unlike many cooking herbs, fennel is a perennial. The plant is tolerant of droughts, but it will grow better if the soil is kept slightly moist. If it is

grown in an outdoor planter, keep a thin layer of mulch over the soil to help retain moisture. If the fennel is grown inside, check the soil often for moisture.

Like cilantro and dill, fennel forms a taproot early and depends on that taproot for its strength and nutrients. Fennel does not like to be transplanted. If you do transplant a fennel seedling, be careful to transport the taproot with plenty of soil around it to avoid causing damage to it.

Fennel needs plenty of water to reach its full size potential. However, it is susceptible to root rot if the roots are left in too much moisture. To ensure the moisture level is correct, use a container with adequate drainage. If the drainage holes do not drain away from the plant, such as with a double-potted container, the water can still affect the roots once it has drained from the drainage holes. Instead, use a pot that drains to an outer tray or a reservoir bottom that does not stay in contact with the soil. A pot with a reservoir bottom has a receptacle attached to the bottom of the pot to hold the water that drains through small slits in the top section of the pot. The container you choose for fennel should also be deep enough to enable the taproot plenty of room to grow.

Fish emulsion, a natural fertilizer made from liquid fish remains, can be used once every three weeks to fertilize the soil in the container. Use a mild, non-concentrated fish emulsion to avoid burning the roots and stems.

There are several types of fennel, each with its own flavors and uses. Sweet fennel and bronze fennel are perennials, while Florence fennel is an annual. Bronze fennel is sometimes used as an ornamental plant. Sweet fennel is used for its leaves and stems and does not grow an edible bulb. The leaves are added to dishes as a flavoring herb. The stems resemble celery and can be eaten in salads and vegetable dishes. The seeds of the sweet fennel taste like licorice and are used to flavor everything from fish to candy. Florence fennel is used for its leaves and bulbs.

What is referred to as the fennel bulb is not truly a bulb. It is actually the plant's stem. True bulbs grow underground. The fennel bulb resembles an underground bulb and is used in salads and vegetable dishes.

Early in the summer, flowerheads will start to grow. Cut those back, and prune the plant to about 12 inches in height. This keeps the plant growing new leaves that can be harvested for cooking. To collect fennel seeds, cut off the flowerhead and hang it upside down over a flat surface. The seeds will drop and can be dried for later use.

Lavender

Botanical name: *Lavandula*
Common name: Lavender, garden lavender
Family name: *Lamiaceae*
Origin: The Mediterranean
Light: Full sun
Size and growth: Up 1-4' in height, up to 2' in width
Minimum temperature: 40° Fahrenheit
Blooming season: Summer to fall
Outside hardiness zone: 4-10

Best time to prune: Spring

Pests or diseases to watch for: Root rot

Fertilizer: Manure

Unique characteristics/growing tips: The soil should be sandy with excellent drainage.

Description:

This perennial is a member of the mint family. There are many varieties of lavender, and each has its own temperature tolerance and will grow to a different size. Small, compact varieties can be grown indoors in containers that can be put onto windowsills or on plant shelves. Munstead, a small variety, grows to about 10 inches in height, small enough for any compact shelf spot. The largest lavender varieties can reach about 3 to 4 feet in height, which makes them more suited to outdoor planters.

Plant a seedling rather than seeds. Lavender plants do not grow well from seeds and can be unpredictable even if they do survive. Seedlings can be

bought in most nurseries during the spring. Once you start growing lavender, you can create new plants through root division, putting the divided plants into new pots, or by creating cuttings from small portions of the plants and re-potting those.

To create the right soil for your container lavender plant, add some sand to your potting soil. Lavender does need regular watering, but the drainage must be extremely good for the plant to avoid moisture damage. Sand aids in the soil's drainage and keeps the soil from retaining too much moisture. Ground limestone can also be helpful in lavender soil. Mulch should not be used on the soil of a lavender pot. Mulch traps in too much moisture for lavender plants and can cause diseases such as root rot.

Lavender has an enormous amount of indoor and outdoor uses. Its fragrance has been favored for thousands of years for its soothing and pleasant nature. Studies have shown lavender's scent does have a calming effect. Many people grow lavender just for this smell and keep a plant or two in the house to scent the air. The flowers can also be dried and used in sachets.

Lavender is used in closets to keep away insects that can destroy clothing. The scent of lavender oil repels many household insects, including moths. This smells better than using mothballs and does not require toxic chemicals to do the job. Lavender is not toxic, but its oil is not edible.

Lavender is a good plant to grow if you want to have continuous access to the fresh flowers for sachets and potpourri. It is also less expensive than buying mothballs every year. Dried lavender can be used in craft projects and arrangements of dried flowers.

If you have a problem with deer or other animals eating your outdoor plants, place a pot of lavender next to those plants to keep animals away. Most of them shy away from the smell and likely will not venture past the lavender to eat your plants. Lavender is not susceptible to most garden pests.

Mint

Botanical name: *Mentha*
Common name: Mint, peppermint, lemon mint, pennyroyal, spearmint
Family name: *Lamiaceae*
Origin: Europe, Asia, and the Mediterranean
Light: Full sun to partial sun
Size and growth: ½" to 3' in height
Minimum temperature: Varies with the specific mint variety

Blooming season: Summer to fall

Outside hardiness zone: 3-11, dependent upon mint variety

Best time to prune: Late summer

Pests or diseases to watch for: Rust, aphids, spider mites

Fertilizer: Organic fertilizer

Unique characteristics/growing tips: Mint is hardy and invasive.

Description:

The mint family includes hundreds of plant varieties, not all of which are edible. The smallest plants in the mint family, Corsican mint, only reach

about half an inch in height and are used as ground cover. The largest mint plants, including peppermint, are edible and are used in everything from toothpastes to herbal medicines.

Like many plants, mint plants can be attacked by aphids and spider mites. These pests can be conquered with a strong dousing of water if the plant is large and kept outside. If you have small, indoor mint plants, try wiping away the pests or cutting off the portions of the plant that are infested.

Rust is a fungal infection that can affect the leaves of mint plants. If you see brown spots on the underside of the leaves, cut off those leaves to stop the spread of the fungus. To prevent it from coming back, adjust the moisture in the pot, allowing the soil to become dry in between waterings.

Keeping mint plants in containers is one of the best ways to grow these plants because they can be extremely invasive, which means a single mint plant can lead to a garden full of mint if you are not careful. When growing mint in containers, give tall mint plants plenty of room or provide stakes for the taller stems. If a mint stem trails over into another pot, it can root there, disrupt the other plant and compete for its moisture and nutrients. Mint should not be planted in the same container with any other plant.

The temperature the plant will tolerate depends on the variety. Some mints will tolerate frost and others should be taken outside only after all risk of frost has passed. Most mint varieties are extremely hardy and need little care to thrive. The soil should be kept slightly moist unless there is a fungus problem. The soil can be fertilized with compost or another gentle organic fertilizer in the spring. However, mint is notoriously hardy and generally does not need to be fertilized unless growth slows.

Bergamot mint has a citrusy flavor and is often used in teas and to calm nausea and alleviate stomach aches. Forest mint is used to calm stomachs and to provide aromatherapy benefits. Apple mint is used to make jelly and as an herbal flavoring. Pennyroyal is a common mint type that is poisonous.

Growing mint at home without the aid of poisonous chemicals means you can grab a leaf and put it in your drink anytime you want. You can also pluck a leaf, crush it, and take in the smell anytime you feel nauseated or anxious. The smell of mint is soothing, good for digestion, and even reduces pain. It can be applied to the gums to alleviate a toothache or eaten to soothe menstrual cramps.

Oregano

Botanical name: *Origanum vulgare*

Common name: Oregano, marjoram

Family name: *Lamiaceae*

Origin: Asia, Europe, and the Mediterranean

Light: Full sun to partial shade

Size and growth: Up to 30" in height, up to 18" in width

Minimum temperature: 45° Fahrenheit

Blooming season: Summer

Outside hardiness zone: 4-9

Best time to prune: During early growth

Pests or diseases to watch for: Aphids, spider mites

Fertilizer: Diluted mineral fertilizer can be used, though this can take away from the flavor of the leaves.

Unique characteristics/growing tips: This hardy plant prefers sandy soil.

Description:

Most oregano plants grow to about 12 inches in height, which makes them convenient and compact container plants. These compact varieties require a pot about 12 inches in diameter to accommodate the plant's growth. Some of the large oregano varieties can grow to 2 feet in height or taller. These larger varieties can also grow wide enough to make them difficult to grow indoors. Outdoor planters can accommodate a large, bushy oregano plant. Outdoor oregano plants generally need to be brought in during freezes. The pot or planter should not be placed in an area that will receive high winds.

You can plant oregano either by germinating seeds or by root division of existing plants. Once established, oregano plants do not care for high

humidity levels. If you are indoors, this is likely not a problem. If you are growing container oregano outdoors in a humid area or in a greenhouse, allow each oregano plant plenty of space so air can circulate around the plant, which negates some of the humidity.

Most oregano species prefer full sunlight, but hot climates can make oregano wilt under full sun. If you live in a hot climate and want to place your container outside, consider placing it so that it will get shade in the afternoon. If you grow oregano indoors, full sunlight through a window is generally fine.

Oregano plants are not highly picky about their soil and are generally hardy plants. However, sandy soils are preferable for this herb. Adding a handful of sand into the potting soil and mixing it before planting oregano seeds or a seedling should give the soil the right consistency.

As an oregano plant grows taller, pruning it to keep it bushy and round will ensure it does not get too leggy and will grow plenty of leaves that can be used in cooking. Fertilize your oregano with a gentle, balanced mineral fertilizer. Too much fertilizer can rob oregano leaves of their flavor.

If aphids or spider mites become a problem, wipe them away with a wet cloth or snip away any infested leaves. Do not use a hose or water stream to wash away pests. Oregano plants are not strong enough to withstand any blast of water focused enough to wipe out the pests.

Oregano is a staple in many Italian, Greek, and Mexican dishes. Some gardeners keep fresh oregano on hand to flavor their pasta sauces, pizza sauce, and meat dishes. It can also be used in salads along with other herbs such as fennel. There are many different varieties of this herb, and each has a different taste. Home gardeners should try out many different varieties to find their favorite type.

Grocery stores usually carry Greek oregano in its dried form. It has a spicy flavor often used in Mexican cooking. Marjoram, another common ingredient in cooking, is a sweet oregano variety. Sicilian oregano has a strong aroma and is often used in Italian cooking and pizza.

Parsley

Botanical name: *Petroselinum crispum*

Common name: Parsley

Family name: *Apiaceae*

Origin: Europe and the Mediterranean

Light: Full sun to partial shade

Size and growth: Up to 18" in height

Minimum temperature: 40° Fahrenheit

Blooming season: Summer

Outside hardiness zone: 5-9

Best time to prune: When seed stems grow

Pests or diseases to watch for: Parsley worms, slugs

Fertilizer: Granulated

Unique characteristics/growing tips: Plants produce 3' seed stalks and need moist soil.

Description:

Parsley is a biennial plant rather than a true annual or perennial. The plants live for two years and require both years to complete their growth and life cycle.

Parsley seeds can be difficult to germinate, which makes many gardeners turn to seedlings to start their parsley plants. Seedlings should be planted in pots that are 12 inches in diameter to house the mature plant. If germinating parsley seeds, use a soilless seed starter that has been moistened and placed in the sunlight. Seeds can be started in seed pots or flats and transplanted into larger pots later.

The plant grows best when it has full sun, but in hot, sunny climates, it might need partial shade during the hottest parts of the day. If your parsley container is indoors, place it near a window that gets full sunlight at least five hours of each day or use a UV light during the day. With enough light, one parsley plant will produce new leaves for six to nine months of the year.

Parsley is non-invasive and can be planted in a container with other plants. Parsley is tolerant of poor soils, but a rich soil with plenty of organic material, such as most high-quality potting soils, is best for growing large and healthy parsley plants. Mix in some slow-acting, granular fertilizer when planting your parsley. The soil should be kept moist, so make sure the container has excellent drainage to prevent too much water from rotting the roots and stems. A light layer of mulch can help keep the soil moist if the pot is kept outside.

When the leaf stems begin to produce three segments, the parsley can be harvested for its tasty leaves. Cut off the outside leaves first when harvesting to ensure that the interior leaves will grow into mature leaves. To make the plant bushier, only pick the leaf segment in the middle of each of the leaf stems.

Parsley should be cut and used immediately for the strongest flavor. It can also be dried for later use. Dried parsley leaves are good for about a year. Alternatively, freeze the leaves to retain more of the flavor. The frozen leaves are good for about six months.

If you keep your parsley outside, caterpillars can be a problem. Parsley worms are a type of butterfly larvae that feed on the leaves of parsley plants. If you find them on your parsley leaves, you can simply pick them off the plant. Container gardening makes it easy to simply bring your plant inside if you find it overrun with parsley worms.

Slugs are another potential problem for parsley grown outdoors. If you have a slug problem, place the pot away from the ground if possible. This removes the moist places slugs look for. An elevated pot might get a stray slug or two, but it will not suffer the damage a parsley plant placed on the ground often does.

When your parsley starts to grow tall flower stalks, prune them to prevent too much height and slowed leaf growth. The stalks flower and then produce seeds, and those stalks can get three times taller than the plant, which makes them awkward indoors. If the stalks are allowed to go to seed, there will be fewer leaves to harvest. If the plant is kept in hot weather, it might go to seed the first year. If kept indoors, it will generally go to seed in the second year.

The leaves of the parsley plant are used as a flavoring for many foods, including omelets, Italian dishes, soups, and salads. It is also a traditional plate garnish. Eating parsley can freshen your breath, and it is full of vitamin C, several B vitamins, and vitamin A.

There are several types of parsley divided into flat-leaf parsley and curly-leaf parsley categories. Curly-leaf parsley varieties are often used as the little plate garnishes common in restaurants. Flat-leaf parsley varieties have the strongest flavors.

Rosemary

Botanical name: *Rosmarinus officinalis*

Common name: Rosemary

Family name: *Lamiaceae*

Origin: The Mediterranean

Light: Full sun to partial shade

Size and growth: 3-6' in height, up to 5' in width

Minimum temperature: 25° Fahrenheit

Blooming season: Spring through summer

Outside hardiness zone: 7-10

Best time to prune: Summer

Pests or diseases to watch for: Powdery mildew, spider mites, aphids

Fertilizer: Liquid kelp

Unique characteristics/growing tips: Rosemary is perfect for topiaries and should be pruned often.

Description:

Rosemary seeds can be hard to start, with a slow germinating time and a low germination rate, which means many seeds do not develop into plants. However, the plant grows well from cuttings. To start a rosemary plant, you can take a small cutting of an adult plant and place the stem into a glass of water in a windowsill until the cutting sprouts roots. Then, move the cutting into a container of potting soil.

You can also use a rooting hormone to make your cut stem sprout roots. Gardening stores and nurseries usually sell these hormones. Dip the cutting

into the hormone and then root it directly into a container of potting soil or into a seed starting mixture. If you choose the seed-starting mixture, the cutting will need to be moved into potting soil once it has established some roots.

Most rosemary plants flower in the spring and early summer, but there are also winter-blooming varieties. Rosemary flowers can be light blue, dark blue, pink, and white in color. The flowers as well as the leaves of the rosemary plant are edible. The flowers can be dried alongside the leaves and used in sachets and potpourri.

Rosemary prefers dry soil and hot conditions. It is hardy and tolerates drought and partial shade and will repel most pests. When conditions are dry, water your outdoor rosemary containers regularly to keep the plant's growth from flagging. If the container is indoors, it should be watered regularly, but the soil does not have to remain moist at all times.

Rosemary grows quickly and is a sturdy plant. This has made it a favorite for creating container topiaries or ornamental shrubs. To create one, simply prune your rosemary into the desired shape and reshape it often during the spring. Spirals are interesting shapes that can be created with a tall rosemary plant. A rosemary plant can also be shaped into an oval, a Christmas tree, or any other visually interesting shape you would like to display. Try keeping the topiary in a container next to the front door or at the bottom of the front steps to add visual interest to your house. Some people create two rosemary topiaries that are then placed on either side of a door or bottom step.

Rosemary can be potted with other plants to create a mini-garden in a large container. Because rosemary grows upward in stalks, it can be planted with shorter plants for an interesting contrast within the container.

You can add a small amount of liquid kelp to the water given to your rosemary plant once or twice a month to keep the foliage strong.

Because of the small leaves and the bushy nature of rosemary plants, it can be difficult to get rid of aphids and spider mites when they infest a plant. You might not be able to reach all of the infested areas to clip them off, and wiping them away can be physically difficult. Insecticidal soap is sometimes needed to rid the rosemary of these pests.

Powdery mildew is a white mildew that looks like powder sprinkled on the leaves of the plant. This mildew usually occurs because the plant does not have enough air circulation. Clip off any leaves infected by the mildew and move the container away from other plants. If you do not have room to move the plant to a spot with plenty of air around it, use a table fan to supply it with a constant airflow to prevent the growth of more mildew.

Rosemary comes in a number of varieties big and small. Some are large bushes that can grow to 4 feet in height. These develop thick, woody stems and can be difficult to keep indoors because of their size and weight. Smaller varieties, such as blue boy, are more suited to small, indoor plant containers.

Rosemary has a sweet smell that has made it an indoor and outdoor favorite for centuries. The herb can be used to flavor fish, meat, vegetable dishes, sauces, and breads. The plants are also useful as ornamental container plants inside or on a porch or patio. The sweet smell can travel across a garden, which gives even a non-flowering garden a nice fragrance. Once picked, rosemary leaves can be dried to use later or frozen to retain some of their texture.

In addition to its culinary uses, rosemary is also used in beauty products. It is often found in shampoos, herbal soaps, and lotions. The pleasant smell of rosemary leaves gives these products a lingering fragrance that has kept it a popular beauty and toiletry ingredient. People who make homemade soaps often grow their own rosemary to keep the fresh herb available at all times.

Sage

Botanical name: *Salvia officinalis*

Common name: Sage, garden sage

Family name: *Lamiaceae*

Origin: The Mediterranean

Light: Full sun

Size and growth: Up to 3' in height, up to 3' in width

Minimum temperature: 10° Fahrenheit

Blooming season: Mid-summer

Outside hardiness zone: 3-11

Best time to prune: Spring

Pests or diseases to watch for: Powdery mildew, spider mites

Fertilizer: Organic fertilizer

Unique characteristics/growing tips: This hardy plant has unusual leaf colors.

Description:

Sage is one of the best herbs that can be grown in a container. It is hardy, does not need to be fertilized often, and will thrive in a variety of soil and light conditions. It does not need to be watered often and thrives best if left alone in a sunny place. Allow the soil to dry out between waterings to avoid giving it too much water. Over-watering is one of the fastest killers of sage.

Sage plants will generally repel pests, but like most garden plants, they can be attacked by aphids and spider mites. If your sage becomes infested,

wiping away the pests is generally the best pest-control method. If that does not work, an insecticidal soap can be used on the infected areas. An insecticidal soap made from peppermint oil or another natural essential oil can repel insects without making the sage toxic to eat.

Potting soil generally provides enough nutrients for sage plants. Sage does not mind being re-potted, so starting it in a small container is fine. If you want to add fertilizer, you can add compost or another organic fertilizer when the plant is being re-potted. Sage plants are not highly picky about their soil, but like most plants, they do require good drainage.

Sage plants are hard to grow from seed. They are generally propagated by dividing the existing plants or by root cuttings. It is best to cut from plants that have new growth areas. These cuttings will then grow rapidly and can start rooting quickly when placed into soil.

Deadhead, or remove the flowerheads from the plant, the sage as soon as you can tell the flowers are dead. Taking off the dead blooms will encourage the plant to make more. This is also a good time for pruning the plant. Pruning and deadheading keep sage bushy rather than leggy. A bushy shape is more convenient for containers and many sage growers find it more attractive.

Sage comes in so many varieties that every herb gardener tends to have his or her favorite type. Sage varieties come with green, yellow, silver, blue, purple, gray, and golden leaves. You might even decide to grow sage for its interesting colors instead of its culinary uses. Indoors, sage adds decoration and a pleasant smell to any container garden. Outdoors, a container of sage will attract butterflies.

Sage is known for its dramatic culinary effect on meats of all types. It is also widely used in rice dishes. Sage is used to make sage tea, a traditional Chinese drink. Many gardeners come up with their own herbal blends to add to their dishes, and sage is often one of the components. It can be used in herbal blends for salad dressings, stir-fry dishes, and more.

Dried sage is often kept in a home for craft projects and for other uses. You can use dried sage to make wreaths and other dried-plant projects. Sage is also used in smudge sticks. By bundling several dried sage stems together and tying them with string, you can create your own smudge stick to dispel negative energy from your home.

Thyme

Botanical name: *Thymus vulgaris*
Common name: Thyme
Family name: *Lamiaceae*
Origin: The Mediterranean
Light: Full sun
Size and growth: 2-18" in height
Minimum temperature: -20° Fahrenheit

Blooming season: Spring and summer

Outside hardiness zone: 4-11

Best time to prune: As needed

Pests or diseases to watch for: Ants, spider mites, fungal rot, mold

Fertilizer: Organic fertilizer

Unique characteristics/growing tips: Thyme prefers dry soil. There are more than 300 varieties available.

Description:

Thyme is so diverse that growers can choose a type of thyme based on specific colors, sizes, and scents.

Thyme grows easily from seeds when the soil is kept moist until the seeds begin sprouting. It also grows well from transplanted seedlings and from cuttings. The plant is hardy overall, with little care needed other than providing plenty of sunlight. Thyme prefers dry soil, so make sure that the container has plenty of drainage. If left in overly moist soil, thyme can rot or develop mold on its leaves and stems. Adding a handful of sterile sand to potting soil can give the soil better drainage and keep it drier.

Thyme does not need frequent fertilization. Strong fertilizers or frequent fertilization can weaken the plant's aroma. To keep the aroma intact, fertilize in April and use an organic fertilizer such as compost or peat moss. Alternatively, apply a small amount of liquid plant food to the thyme.

Thyme does not need regular pruning to steer growth, but you can prune any new growth to keep the plant your preferred size. You only need to prune the plant to remove a dead stem or a dead flowerhead. If you do prune the new growth areas to keep the plant shorter and bushier, the leaves and stems that are cut can be frozen and later used in cooking.

The smallest thyme varieties, called creeping thymes, grow to about 2 to 3 inches in height. These flowering thymes are used as ornamental plants and can be used as a soil cover in pots with taller plants. Common thyme grows to about 6 to 10 inches in height. When kept alone in a container as an ornamental plant, a thyme variety with a variegated leaf, or a leaf displaying multiple colors, might give you the most visual interest.

Growing thyme gives you instant access to the fresh herb for use in sauces and to flavor poultry, stew, red meat, and various side dishes. You can also grow the herb simply for its pleasant scent. Thyme leaves and stems can be eaten at any time. Simply cut off the portion you need and use it in your recipe. The flowers are also edible.

Common thyme has a light scent similar to parsley. This variety is most often used for cooking purposes. Some other varieties have a lemony scent. Most varieties of thyme are evergreen and perennial, which gives thyme growers access to the leaves year round. The leaves come in different shades of green as well as green-and-yellow or white-and-yellow-variegated leaves. Depending on the thyme variety, the flowers can be deep purple, white, pink, or lavender.

Great Herb Garden Combinations

With so many herbs, it is necessary to narrow down the thousands of varieties available to a manageable number you will use or simply enjoy having around. You will also need to assess your space, lighting, and needs when planning your garden.

If you have a space issue, growing a few of the smallest herbs together in one or two pots can create a useful herb garden that takes up little space. Small herbs include cilantro, parsley, thyme, and fernleaf dill.

You might also need a combination of herbs if you have little sunlight coming into your home and you need the containers to stay indoors. Lemon balm, mint, oregano, and Dukat dill will all grow in partial shade.

If the herbs are intended for a specific use, such as for certain recipes or natural remedies, this can shape the eventual herb garden. Planning for several herbs that complement each other's uses can be a practical way to decide which varieties to use.

Most herbs have fragrant leaves, but not all of those scents work well together. Choosing herbs with complementary scents can enhance the smell of your herb garden instead of creating an overwhelming cacophony of smells. For example, a large container can hold several young herb plants that have lemon scents, such as lemon thyme, lemon balm, and lemon basil. Herbs that have light scents, such as parsley or oregano, can be planted together with stronger-smelling plants such as rosemary or chamomile.

Italian cooking garden

A number of herbs are traditionally used in Italian dishes. These are often grown together in an herb container garden by gardeners who love authentic Italian cooking. You can grow these herbs in clusters of small pots on a shelf or baker's rack. Also, herb pot holders hold several small pots in a straight or pyramid arrangement to conserve space.

Italian cooking usually includes a rich sauce liberally flavored with herbs. Having these fresh herbs available at all times can give these sauces a new dimension of flavor. Italian cooking herbs include basil, fennel, sage, oregano, rosemary, and parsley. All of these can be used not only in Italy's famous sauces but also to flavor fish and meat dishes.

Oregano and basil are often used together, such as in most tomato-based pasta sauces. Basil is often used in sauces, soups, and marinades, particularly tomato-based and pesto sauces. Sweet Italian large leaf basil is the type most often used in Italian sauces, and Genovese basil is also commonly used. Oregano is used in salads and meat and fish dishes in addition to its use in sauces. Basil and oregano both grow best in full sun and can be grown side by side in a window.

The distinctive flavor of Italian sausage and meatballs comes in part from fennel seeds. Fennel seeds can also be used in meat and fish dishes. In addition to the seeds, the bulb of the fennel plant is added to many Italian dishes.

Many dishes also call for the distinctive flavor of rosemary, which can be used fresh or dried. It is traditionally used in lamb and focaccia as well as with roasted vegetables. Sage is used in saltimbocca, a Mediterranean veal dish, salads, and meat dishes. Parsley is used in sauces, stews, potato dishes, and garnishes.

Kitchen garden

A kitchen garden, a type of garden used to grow plants you will use in cooking, usually includes parsley, thyme, sage, rosemary, chives, and any specialty herbs you use frequently. To get an idea of which herbs you use regularly, take a look at the dried herbs you already own. These are likely herbs you bought to go with recipes and the ones you will be using again in the future.

Sometimes, having a kitchen garden actually spurs the gardener to start cooking more dishes from scratch. For other gardeners, the kitchen garden simply replaces the dried herbs that were once bought from the grocery store. Growing your own herbs saves money on expensive dried herbs and delivers a more satisfying cooking experience.

To make things as convenient as possible, some people choose to place their kitchen garden in the kitchen rather than in a separate room or scattered throughout the home. You can keep the garden in an herb pot container that holds a number of small plant pots. Alternatively, you can group several separate pots together on a countertop or windowsill. If your kitchen has a window, growing the plants can be as easy as putting them near the window and keeping the plants watered.

Without a window or with a small window that does not bring in direct sunlight, the herbs can be grown under a plant light. To make plants and lights manageable in the kitchen, the lights can be installed on the underside of kitchen cabinets and the pots placed on the countertop under the cabinets. This use of space keeps the plants close by when you are cooking and keeps them from taking up a large amount of kitchen space.

Medicinal garden

You might chose to grow a medicinal garden, a garden with a variety of herbs used for medicinal purposes. Most herbs have medicinal uses that have been passed down for centuries. Some of these medicinal uses have been proven by modern medical studies, and some still have only anecdotal evidence to recommend them.

For people who prefer herbal remedies or take herbal supplements regularly, a medicinal herb garden is both useful and cost effective. Many herbs are used to make herbal teas, others are ingested without any preparation, and some are used only topically to treat skin problems. Although herbs taken orally do not always taste great by themselves or in teas, they can be flavored with honey or a slice of lemon to make the taste more palatable. The following are some herbs you might grow in your medicinal garden:

- Sweet basil is used in herbal teas to treat indigestion. Its oil is used topically to treat sore muscles.

- Chamomile is also used to make tea. It has a calming effect and is used to help treat anxiety and insomnia. It can be used topically to treat rough patches of skin.

- Coriander can be used in tea for the same effects as chamomile.

- Mint can be used as an herbal flavoring for tea. It is used to clear phlegm and make other herbal remedies smell or taste better. To loosen phlegm, mint leaves are crushed and placed into boiling water. This releases the scent of the leaves into the air and acts as a natural decongestant.

- St. John's wort is a popular herb that can be used for treating depression. Studies have shown that though it is not always effective for treating major depression, it is as effective for treating mild to moderate depression as prescription medications, and in some cases, it is even more effective than those medications. It was found to have fewer side effects than many prescription drugs. The herb is also used as a mild sedative. The plant is a perennial shrub that reaches 1 to 3 inches in height.

- Thyme is not only indispensable in a kitchen garden, it is also useful in a medicinal garden. The herb is used to treat sore throats and coughing.

- Chewing feverfew leaves is said to treat headaches. It is also made into an herbal tea to treat fevers.

- Angelica is used in herbal teas to stimulate circulation and boost energy. It has been shown to have antibacterial properties and is often used to treat fevers, coughs, stomach problems, and colds. It is also used to create an herbal gargling solution that treats sore mouths and throats. Some people also use the root topically to treat acne. Angelica is a tall perennial plant, which grows as high as 10 feet.

- Valerian is often grown for the medicinal properties of its roots. The roots can be used as an anxiety treatment and a mild sedative. It is used in commercial sleeping pills. When used in an herbal cream, it can be applied topically to treat rashes and acne. Valerian is a flowering herb that grows to about 4 inches in height. It can produce white or pink flowers.

- Calendula is a flowering herb used to make creams and mouthwash. Both are made with the flowers of the plant. The flowers are steeped in water to make a natural mouthwash. The flower petals are used to make topical creams to treat small skin wounds.

- Echinacea, also known as purple coneflower, is a flowering plant used to make herbal teas that treat various illnesses by boosting the immune system. It is also used to treat psoriasis, eczema, and other skin conditions as well as arthritis.

- Common yarrow is used in herbal teas to treat colds and fevers. The flower petals can be used topically in creams to treat small skin wounds.

- Hyssop is used in herbal teas to treat colds and sore throats.

Many of these herbs are small enough to be grown in indoor containers. Some, such as St. John's wort, grow into larger plants that can be kept small by frequent pruning. Others like Echinacea, which grows as tall as 4 feet in height, will grow well in containers but might be impractical indoors.

Common Mistakes to Avoid when Growing Herbs

Growing herbs requires being attentive to the needs of the plants. Check their leaves and stems to make sure they are healthy and free of pests. Watch for any discoloration and feel the soil often to ensure the plant has the optimal conditions for its health and growth.

When growing herbs in containers, make sure that you choose varieties that are small enough to keep in your containers. Although most herbs have one or more compact varieties, many also have enormous varieties that can top 6 feet in height. If you want to grow rosemary, sage, or another plant that has dozens of varieties, choose carefully or you might find that you do not have space for the mature plant.

Be conscious of herb variety names. Some plant families, such as the carrot family, have a number of edible and inedible herbs in them. Just because a plant is in the carrot family does not mean that it will grow carrots.

Be aware of the plant's growth pattern. Some herbs must be pruned to keep them a manageable size for containers. Many herbs, such as sage, rosemary, oregano, and thyme, develop thick, woody stems over time if they are not pruned correctly. These thick stems do not produce the leaves and stems used in cooking or herbal remedies. Thick stems also mean the plant must grow outward in width to keep the plant producing the leaves and flowers gardeners want to harvest. This leads to a much wider, larger, and less attractive plant.

To prevent woody stems, prune the plants in the spring when new growth is at its height. Cut away any dead stems to keep the plant as compact as possible and to encourage the growth of new stems. The size of some plants, such as rosemary, can also be contained by trimming off part of the plant's roots. This is done by pulling the plant out of the soil and trimming the sides and bottom of its root ball. This can be done whenever the plant grows larger than you want it to be, and it will not harm the plant.

Avoid pruning herbs in the fall when the plants are going dormant for the winter. Pruning will encourage the plant to create new leaves and stems instead of going into its natural dormancy. This process can disrupt the plant's natural growth cycles as well as create too much growth in the plant. Dormancy usually starts in late fall and is a natural function that keeps the plant from growing new leaves and stems during cold weather when the young growth would be most susceptible to the cold.

Most herbs do not have serious problems with plant pests and diseases and are hardy as long as their basic needs are met. However, aphids can be a problem for basil, chamomile, fennel, mint, coriander, oregano, rosemary, sage, and other herbs. When you see a cluster of small, moving dots on a plant, it might be infested with aphids. These bugs tend to gather around new growth areas as well as the very top of a plant. Aphids can be a problem inside as well as outside.

If you find aphids, remove the infested plant immediately before the pests can spread to other plants. Cut off the infested areas of the plant if possible and leave the plant in isolation until you are sure there are no more aphids on the plant. Inspect plants regularly to look for pests, which will ensure any problem can be stopped before it spreads. If only a few aphids or other pests are present, try to simply pick them off to end the infestation.

Unless you are growing herbs only to have a nice fragrance in the air, avoid using poisons on them to get rid of pests. Many herbs, such as chamomile and lavender, emit a smell that repels bugs, and these can be used alongside plants that are susceptible to insect invasion to keep the garden safer.

Sometimes, you can plant an insect repellent such as chamomile in the same container as other herbs. You can also place a pot of chamomile in the center of other pots filled with various herbs that are susceptible to pests.

Using organic fertilizers can help keep pests at bay. Organic fertilizers use natural soil nutrients to boost plant growth. Artificial fertilizers often create growth that is faster than what occurs in nature. This fast growth can leave the plant unable to fight off the damage caused by pests. With the plant's energy so engaged in growth, it has little energy left over for fighting damage and injury. The abundance of new growth is also a powerful attractant for large quantities of aphids. Artificial fertilizers and quick growth can also dilute the natural flavors of the herbs.

Getting too much water is a major problem for many herbs. Too much water can lead to root and stem rot and mildew on the stems and leaves. This is often the fastest killer of herbs, and it can be avoided. To keep from watering herbs too often, stick to a regular watering schedule. This might take some time to put into place as you observe how long it takes each plant's soil to become dry. Each plant will have its own timetable for watering.

To further ensure the plant is not sitting in too much moisture, plant herbs in potting soil and fertilize with organic materials instead of planting them directly into peat moss or another fertilizer. Potting soil contains substances that provide the soil better drainage and allow the moisture to be released from the soil slowly rather than all at once.

The type of drainage used is also important to the herbs. If you have many small pots with drainage on the outside, try placing those pots on a tray that can handle an overflow of water. This provides a healthy way to allow excess water to leave the pot. Although most pots have drainage holes, if excess water sits in contact with the drainage holes, the plant is still absorbing that water. Many times, a plant is placed into a pot with drainage, and that pot is placed into a larger pot that holds the excess liquid. Although double potting an herb does allow for some drainage, it actually keeps the drainage water in contact with the soil. If you use this potting arrangement for herbs, check the outer pot regularly to make sure the inside pot is not sitting in drained water.

You can also plant herbs that do not require moist soil in a pot that has a drainage reservoir at the bottom. Generally, these pots are priced similarly to regular plant pots, and they keep the drainage water away from the plant's soil. In the reservoir system, the water drains to a separate compartment under the soil where it can be either removed from the pot or allowed to evaporate over time.

If a plant's leaves begin to become discolored with brown or yellow spots, the soil might not have enough nutrients. This does not happen as often with herbs as with more finicky plants, but it is possible. It usually occurs if an herb has been sitting in the same soil for a long period of time. The plant likely needs an infusion of nutrients in the form of an organic fertilizer.

If a plant grows slowly during the spring and summer, particularly when the plant has not yet developed seeds, it might not have enough sunlight. Experiment with new areas for the plant and note whether the plant begins to speed up the growth of new stems and leaves.

If an herb begins producing seeds before it should, it might be in conditions that are too hot. If the plant begins developing flowers before its blooming season, the production of new leaves will slow down or even stop. This means fewer leaves that can be used for your cooking or medicinal purposes. If this happens, move the plant to an area that gets less sunlight and cut off the flowers before they produce seeds.

CASE STUDY:
STRAIGHT FROM THE EXPERT

Kerry Michaels
About.com's Guide to
Container Gardening
containergardening.guide@about.com
www.containergardening.about.com
Phone: (207) 233-8555

I grow a large container garden of edibles each year. Peppers and cucumbers are planted in galvanized trash cans; tomatoes go in a big water trough; carrots, lettuces, and herbs — dill and chives are family favorites — fill every available flowerpot and planter.

Container gardening gives you more control over your growing conditions. You can create the perfect soil mix for your plants without a lot of effort; you can move plants in and out of the sun as needed, and you can bring tender plants indoors for the winter. Plus, if you move, your plants can go with you.

Growing food indoors is a great way to extend the growing season. It is also a way to try your hand at growing foods you would not normally be able to grow in your area — things such as citrus fruits and bananas.

Once you have determined which plants will grow in containers, the best plants to grow are the ones you like best — your favorite foods and your favorite flowers.

Growing your own food is a way to save money and gain control over what you are eating. People are realizing they can take the money that they would spend on a single tomato and use it instead to buy a tomato plant that will provide a whole season of tomatoes.

When you shop for produce at the grocery store, you are limited by how much you can afford to buy. When you grow your own food, you are limited only by how much you are able to grow. Even a few containers can produce a tremendous bounty, and you do not have to pay for that bounty by the pound.

Chapter 8

GROWING VEGETABLES IN CONTAINERS

Growing vegetables is an activity most people associate with a farm or with a large plot of land. However, neither is necessary for growing a variety of tasty and nutritious vegetables. Many vegetables can be grown in containers, and growing them in containers can actually prevent many of the common problems associated with growing vegetables in the ground.

So many dwarf and miniature varieties of vegetables exist that it is possible to grow vegetables in very small pots and still expect a nice harvest of edibles. A miniature carrot plant can grow tiny carrots for salads and snacks in a compact space. Miniature squash, bell pepper, and cucumber plants produce small versions of these vegetables from a small plant that can be grown indoors.

Even full-size vegetables can be grown indoors if the space is available. Climbing vegetable plants such as peas, zucchini, cucumbers, beans, and squash can be grown indoors with a trellis to take on most of the bulk of the plant. This allows the plant to take up vertical space instead of overtaking the floor or countertops.

Some plants, such as lettuce and carrots, are compact in their full-size forms. They can be grown in a corner or a room and not take up any more space than some compact, miniature vegetable plants.

Growing salad greens in containers is a popular type of container gardening. A small garden of salad greens does not take up much space, and it allows for a wider variety of greens than most grocery stores carry. With a few small containers, salad fans can grow lettuce, parsley, kale, spinach, radishes, and mustard greens and have enough available to create a number of different salad combinations.

You can also use outdoor containers to grow your vegetables in some of the best possible conditions. Not only do outdoor containers get all the benefits of the sunlight and warm temperatures of the spring and summer, they also get the controlled soil composition of potting soil and limited exposure to predators. Although rabbits readily consume garden vegetables in many areas, they cannot access a raised container that puts the vegetables above their reach.

Large planters can grow several vegetables at the same time. By putting two or three vegetables together that have the same sunlight, soil, and water needs, you save space and create a garden that is easily watered and checked for pests.

Can You Really Grow Vegetables in Containers?

Many vegetables grow very well in containers. In many areas, vegetables can grow far better in containers than they would in the ground. For example, if you have inhospitable soil, some vegetables will grow more easily in containers than they would in the ground. Vegetables generally need soil that has plenty of organic material and good drainage. Good potting soil will provide both of these.

Potting soil and additives give you far more control over the soil quality and pH than you would have if you planted your vegetables directly in the ground. This can translate into better health and larger growth for your vegetables. Using potting soil also allows you to fertilize and add nutrients more easily than if the plants were in the ground.

With container-grown vegetables, you can be assured of the container's drainage — something not always apparent in the ground soil. If the containers are indoors, you also have far more control in protecting your plants from pests. With enough care, you can keep pests out altogether. Caterpillars and snails, the bane of many vegetables that grow outdoors, are not likely to plague an indoor garden. Plants in containers can also be placed on elevated surfaces to keep the plants away from ground-dwelling pests like snails.

For new vegetable growers, growing vegetables in containers means not taking a risk with their garden. If you are used to growing plants in the ground, you know what a big commitment it can be. You can easily spend a full day tilling, mixing soil, pulling weed seeds, and planting new plants. Container gardening requires much less time. Your only time commitment is simply pouring potting soil into a container and perhaps adding a nutrient or two, depending on the plant variety. Many people who have struggled to find the time to start a garden in the ground can actually create the garden they have dreamed of through container gardening.

Like growing herbs, growing vegetables in containers requires the right type of pots that will allow for proper drainage. Although many vegetables grow well in moist soil, fungal infections are common problems for the plants.

The containers must have bottom drainage to allow excess water to leave the container.

Before choosing the specific container for a vegetable plant, find out what the adult size of the plant will be. Some vegetables are actually roots that require a larger interior space that can hold enough soil to contain the adult vegetables. Potatoes and carrots, for example, are root vegetables that have different space requirements than many vegetables.

Like herbs, most vegetables can be started in seed flats, and the strongest of those young plants can then be transplanted to a larger container. Some vegetables, however, do not transplant well. Lettuce, carrots, and potatoes do not like to be transplanted, and the shock of transplantation might kill the plant or end the growth of the vegetables. For these plants, you should put the young plants or seeds directly into pots large enough for the adult plant.

Because potting soil is formulated to retain water longer than most outdoor soils, potted vegetables might not need watering as often as plants that are growing in the ground. However, if the plant containers are kept outside in the sunlight and heat, it is important to check the soil each day to see whether any moisture is left in the soil. Additionally, outdoor vegetable containers should not be black or dark colored. This dark coloring can raise the temperature of the soil inside the pot. It also raises the temperature of the water inside, which causes the water to evaporate as steam, resulting in damaged roots and leaves.

Because so many vegetable plants are susceptible to molds, fungi, and mildew, growers usually apply water directly to the soil instead of the leaves and stems of the plants.

If you grow vegetables in larger outdoor containers, place a hose onto the soil and let the water flow slowly into the soil. If you have indoor containers, use a watering can and place the spout onto the soil to provide the plant with water.

Why Grow Your Own Vegetables?

Growing your own vegetables allows you to save money, know the exact history of your food, bond with your children and family through the shared activity of planting and harvesting, provide nutrient-rich foods for your household, and experience the joy of growing vegetables.

When you grow your own vegetables, you can choose from more varieties than just the limited few available in the grocery store. Heirloom varieties of many vegetables are not available in most grocery stores, but they are available in seed packets and as seedlings. Heirloom vegetables, which are grown from pure open-pollinated lines of seeds, are more flavorful than the hybridized versions generally seen in stores. Many varieties available in stores, such as squash, have been selectively bred with an emphasis on size and the yield of the plant instead of taste.

Growing vegetables is also a fun and rewarding hobby. It is a gentle exercise and a good stress reliever for those who enjoy working with their hands. Container gardening is not strenuous and provides light physical activity. It is also easy enough for children to do right alongside adults.

Growing your own food gives you a clear reward for your efforts. With some effort to create the right conditions for your plants, you have a clear timetable for when your work will come to fruition. Each plant has its own growth and production timetable, which makes it possible for you to plant and expect vegetables on a specific schedule.

Watching seeds sprout in seed flats or containers is an exciting way to see your efforts spring to life. You do not have to be dedicated to gardening to feel a little thrill when you see the seeds sprout and start forming the leaves of your new plants.

Growing your own vegetables is also an ecologically sound practice that allows you to flex your "green" muscles and conserve energy by using less gas and water. Having fresh vegetables growing at home saves the gas you would have used to drive to the store to buy produce.

Because container-grown plants are placed in potting soil that holds onto moisture, you might need less water to keep the plants growing than their commercial counterparts require. And, in containers, the plants face fewer threats from pests and predators, which means they do not need any pesticides that could harm the environment. In containers, weeds are rarely a problem, which makes herbicides unnecessary as well. Growing your vegetables in containers means it is not necessary to alter the local ecosystem to grow them.

When you grow your own vegetables, you always have a fresh supply. This provides you with better nutrition and more flavor in your fresh food than with frozen and canned varieties. Fresh food also takes less time to prepare. Instead of thawing or draining your vegetables, you can simply pluck them from the plants and use them right away.

To save money at the grocery store

When you grow your own produce, you can also expect smaller grocery bills. For some families, it can mean the difference between having fresh produce regularly and having it only as a rare treat. Making the food budget stretch often requires buying vegetables that are frozen, canned, dried, or otherwise processed and prepared. Doing so allows families to purchase more, and it ensures that the produce stays good for a longer period of time.

With fresh, growing vegetables at home, new produce is available as soon as it ripens. Instead of buying produce that has already been picked, you can pick the produce as you need it. This makes it less likely that the items will spoil before they are used. A single plant can produce for a long period of time, so you do not have to purchase vegetables each week. You no longer have to make do with the canned variety to fit your food budget. Instead, fresh vegetables continue to grow throughout the growing season without any additional expenditures.

In 2009, the National Gardening Association estimated a gardener who spends about $70 for gardening supplies and seeds can grow 300 pounds of fresh vegetables that have a retail value of about $600. This represents a savings of more than $500. This figure is based on a 600-square foot garden, so your results will be a bit smaller.

Saving money on vegetables also means there is more money left over for other things, including entertainment. This extra money can change the entire household budget and allow you to afford things that were not possible before.

To know where your food is coming from

The many produce recalls over the last few years have scared some people into growing their own vegetables simply to avoid the threat of dangerous bacteria. Lettuce and spinach have each caused massive product recalls in the last two decades due to salmonella and other bacterial outbreaks. According to *Frozen Food Age,* there have been 20 E. coli outbreaks since 1995 that involved spinach or lettuce. E. coli is a bacterium that can cause diarrhea, vomiting, and serious infections in children and the elderly, which can result in death.

These outbreaks are usually caused by unsanitary conditions when growing or picking the vegetables. By growing produce at home, you control all of the conditions and can ensure the vegetables are handled in a sanitary manner.

If you have ever spent extra money on produce to get items grown with fewer pesticides and herbicides, you know how expensive that can be. But many vegetables, such as bell peppers, spinach, and potatoes, have such high levels of pesticides, it is important to buy organic varieties to avoid consuming any toxins. Bell peppers have some of the highest levels of pesticide use. Spinach has been found to contain traces of DDT as well as the carcinogenic, or potentially cancer-causing, pesticide permethrin. DDT is a banned pesticide believed to cause cancer. It is banned in the United States, but it is still used in less-developed countries, some of which export food to the United States.

For children, pregnant women, and people who have immune deficiencies, the buildup of pesticides on vegetables can cause serious health effects. Pesticides have been shown to cross the placenta of pregnant women and pose a risk to the developing fetus.

When you grow your own vegetables at home in containers, you can do so without any pesticides or herbicides. You are growing organic vegetables that completely circumvent the poisonous environment of most commercial farms. Even organic produce grown without the use of additional pesticides can, and does, absorb traces of pesticides from the soil. This has allowed the long-banned DDT to be absorbed by vegetables that are being sold today in the produce section of your grocery store.

Some produce is imported from foreign countries that do not have the same safety standards as U.S.-grown vegetables. Although some stores are making an effort to tell consumers when something was imported into the United States, many do not. It is impossible to simply look at produce and know where it was grown or what substances it has been exposed to.

To teach your children about growing and science

Growing your own vegetables is a great learning experience for families. Kids who get to see seeds, seedlings, and the strong, growing plants they become will learn a little about botany. Gardening includes many different lessons and potential teaching topics including plant growth, seed germination, and how insects, weeds, and cultivated plants interact together.

There are other lessons to be learned while gardening as well. When growing plants, kids learn how to set and reach goals. Seeing the physical results of their work — the plants and the vegetables they produce — shows children they can be rewarded for their hard work and dedication to a goal.

Because container gardening is not too physically difficult, even young children can help fill pots with soil, mix in fertilizers, and place young plants into the soil. They can also start seeds in seed flats by pressing the seeds into the moistened soil. Many kids check their seeds excitedly each day to see whether they have sprouted. This time is perfect for lessons in seed structure and how the seed develops from a dormant seed into a young plant.

Kids can also try germinating seeds in between wet paper towels. This can become a fun hobby for kids who enjoy gardening and want to grow their own plants. Any type of dried bean can be germinated quickly in a paper towel.

For home-schooled children, botany experiments can become science lessons during school hours. Children can conduct botanical experiments or simply be in charge of their own plants, taking them from seeds or young plants to mature plants that produce vegetables for the family. Gardening can become small, individual science lessons as well as part of unit studies. They can even be used as long-term projects. Experimentation with different soil types and different light levels can show children what conditions plants need to grow as well as teach them the scientific method of investigation.

Growing vegetables at home also helps kids to see where their food actually originates. Assigning one or more plants to the kids to take care of is an enjoyable lesson in responsibility. For example, if you do not water a plant, it will not grow. Plants do not listen to excuses, and kids get to see the cause and effect of their own actions. Responsibility is an important lesson nature can teach.

Kids will learn about nutrition when they see the fresh produce and learn about the pesticides they are avoiding by growing food at home. Children can also learn about nutrition and health by learning about the vitamins and minerals available in each vegetable, such as calcium in red beets, magnesium in broccoli, and iron in squash.

For younger children, gardening at home can help them develop hand-eye coordination. Digging, pressing seeds in the dirt, and re-potting seedlings are activities kids can do to perfect their motor skills.

To put flavorful, nutritious, fresh food at your fingertips

The convenience of having food readily available is another major motivator for home gardeners. If you live far from the nearest grocery store, having vegetables right there on the porch is easier than taking a long trip to the store for a little produce. And even if you are close to a store, it is not always convenient to go shopping whenever you want a piece of cucumber.

Many other factors can make shopping inconvenient. It can be difficult to prepare for a shopping trip and get the shopping done while balancing your family's needs. Busy schedules can make it difficult to get to the store every time the produce drawer runs low.

As busy as people are these days, they often choose their food based on convenience rather than nutritional value. With fresh vegetables at your fingertips, healthy, organic food is within easy reach and as convenient as a fast-food restaurant. Imagine being able to curl up with a good book and a plate of fresh vegetables just picked from the vine. Your garden can change the way you look at convenience food.

Having fresh vegetables at home can help your children make nutritious food choices and provide a healthier alternative for their afternoon snack.

Vegetables are very easy to grow and respond well to containers of all types

As long as you have a high-quality potting soil, an area that gets sunlight, and running water in the house, you can grow vegetables in containers. Most vegetables are hardy plants that do not need much fertilization and will thrive if given the right degree of sunlight and moisture.

Vegetables should be grown in pots that are at least 8 inches in diameter. When growing vegetables in containers, make sure the containers are clean and free of any bacteria or mildew. If the container has been used before, scrub the inside of the container with a weak bleach solution of one-part bleach and nine-parts water. This will kill any bacteria or pests that could infect your new plant.

Plants such as potatoes and cucumbers have larger root systems and require deeper containers than leafy vegetables. The pots for those vegetables should be at least 16 inches deep. A deeper pot can increase the yield of those vegetables. Be sure to check your vegetable's root and growth expectation when deciding which container to buy.

The easiest vegetables to grow in containers are ones that have shallow roots, which take up little space. These include lettuce, spinach, and radishes. Plants like potatoes, squash, and peppers have large root systems that require wider pots to accommodate them. Some dwarf varieties of these plants do exist, such as several varieties of dwarf squash. These are easier to grow in containers.

The early morning is the best watering time for containers kept outdoors. Morning waterings allows the soil to soak up plenty of water before the afternoon sun evaporates the moisture from the leaves. Because the afternoon sun will dry the plant, early watering helps protect the plant from fungal growth as well as moisture-seeking insects.

Most types of vegetable plants require watering every day, particularly if the containers are kept outdoors. Small containers kept indoors might not need watering as often. Most vegetable plants need full sunlight exposure, though leafy greens like spinach, cabbage, and lettuce need shade. One of the advantages of growing your vegetables in containers is that they can be placed in the best spot to receive the amount of sun exposure they need.

If you are in a hurry to start your garden, buying a variety of young plants at the local nursery can help jump-start the garden.

A Complete List of Container-grown Vegetables

Many common vegetables are grown at home because of their versatility in recipes or their usage as convenient snacks. The following are some common vegetables that can be grown in containers indoors or out.

Beans

Botanical name: Varies by variety

Common name: Beans

Family name: *Fabaceae*

Origin: The Americas, Europe, and Asia

Light: Full sun

Size and growth: Varies by variety

Minimum temperature: 60° Fahrenheit

Blooming season: Summer through fall

Outside hardiness zone: 2-11, depending on variety

Best time to prune: Prune dead growth and small flowers

Pests or diseases to watch for: Fungi, aphids, beetles

Fertilizer: Compost or slow-release granules

Unique characteristics/growing tips: To facilitate growth, provide support for climbing bean varieties.

Description:

Many varieties of beans exist, with origins all over the world. Beans are popular everywhere because of their dense nutritional value. They are high in fiber, protein, vitamins, and minerals. This makes them a highly valuable source of nutrition. Beans are also low in calories, which makes them healthy for any diet plan.

When growing beans, you should consider the type of plant you want to grow. Some beans are toxic when eaten raw, and these may not be the best varieties to grow in a family container garden. Runner beans, soybeans, and kidney beans are all poisonous when eaten uncooked. Some beans grow as bushes and others as climbing vines. Climbing beans need to have stakes or lattices provided to give them support. If you do not want to provide supports for a vine or do not have the vertical space, a bush type of bean plant will be best.

Bean plants tend to prefer warm weather and full sun. They should only be taken outdoors a week or two after the area has had its last freeze. Climbing bean plants can tolerate some shade, but they must have direct sunlight for six or more hours each day. When fertilizing bean plants, choose a fertilizer low in nitrogen and high in phosphates. Choose a 1-2-1 fertilizer that is a slow-release variety.

Bush beans and climbing vines both need to have ample air circulation around them. Bean plants are susceptible to fungi and other bean diseases that can be caused by too much moisture and too little air circulation.

The soil should stay moist for most bean plants. Some are drought tolerant, but they will grow and produce better when watered regularly. If the containers are kept outside, a thin layer of bark mulch over the soil can help retain moisture. However, make sure the mulch is not touching the leaves or the stems of the plant. This can keep too much moisture on the plant and cause fungal infections. Indoors, simply check the soil each day and water if it is not moist. Use the soil-watering method — applying water directly to the soil and not the plant — to avoid putting too much moisture on the plant.

Most bean plants take about eight to nine weeks to mature and produce beans. If you want to harvest plenty of beans throughout the growing season, use several bean plants, starting one every two weeks. This will keep beans growing continuously and supply you with enough for recipes, side dishes, and perhaps even extra beans to freeze. Extra beans can also be dried and stored long term.

The type of bean plant you choose to grow will probably have to do with your personal tastes. If you have not tried a broad variety of beans, there are many colors, sizes, and types available that can be grown in a container garden. Common varieties include broad beans, mung beans, cowpeas, garbanzo beans, peas, hyacinth beans, tepary beans, lima beans, runner beans, kidney beans, pinto beans, lentils, velvet beans, coral beans, ricebeans, and many more. If you have thought about trying new beans but are not sure which you would enjoy, grow several varieties during your first growing season and eat each to find your favorites.

Some beans are not edible raw, such as kidney beans and red beans, but others can be eaten right off the vine. Young beans picked before they ripen are tender and tasty raw. More mature beans may need to be soaked and cooked before they are tender enough to eat.

If you are growing kidney or red beans, be sure to cook them for at least ten minutes before eating them. This is long enough to destroy the toxic chemicals within them. If you have children in the house, these might not be the best beans to grow in your container garden.

Carrots

Botanical name: *Daucus carota*

Common name: Carrot

Family name: *Apiaceae*

Origin: The Middle East

Light: Full sun

Size and growth: Varies by variety

Minimum temperature: 65° Fahrenheit

Blooming season: Summer to fall

Outside hardiness zone: 3-11

Best time to prune: No pruning is necessary

Pests or diseases to watch for: Root rot, fungi, flea beetles, wireworms

Fertilizer: Compost

Unique characteristics/growing tips: A deep container is needed for most varieties.

Description:

Carrots are highly nutritious, tasty, and easy to grow if you set up the right conditions. They take up little space above the container, but because carrots are root vegetables, they need to have plenty of space within the container. Although there are some varieties of short, even round, carrots, most are long and thin and require a deep container. Choose a container at least 24 inches deep unless you are growing a miniature carrot variety.

You can easily use a tall trash can or a five-gallon bucket to create a carrot nursery. To use one of these containers, drill holes on the bottom of the container to allow for water drainage. Place the container over a tray or other water collector if the carrots are to be grown indoors. If the container will be indoors, find a sunny window where the top of the container will receive full sunlight.

The vegetable is actually the taproot of the plant. Like many plants that have a thick taproot, carrots do not like to be transplanted. The growth of the carrot might be stunted if transplanted, or the carrot itself might grow into a forked shape. To grow carrots properly, set up a container large enough to hold the mature plant. Fill the container with potting soil and compost or other organic materials, such as peat moss. Then, plant the carrot seeds on top.

Carrot seeds are tiny, so be careful not to plant too many. Carrots should be planted about ¼ inch below the surface of the soil. Press them gently into the top of the soil, or sprinkle them lightly over the soil and then water them so they sink into the soil. Once the seeds start to sprout, thin them to about 2 inches apart.

Young carrot plants need little interference. They should not be fertilized, dug up, or transplanted while the carrots are growing. The more interference they have, the greater the chance that the carrots will be stunted or grow forked or crooked.

Water carrot plants regularly, but make sure the soil has plenty of drainage. As a root vegetable, carrots are susceptible to root rot. When this occurs, your entire carrot crop can be ruined. To avoid this, water your carrots every other day unless the soil still feels moist. The soil does not need to dry out between waterings, but avoid watering the soil again if there is still significant moisture evident in it.

Growing carrots in containers is highly preferable to growing them in the ground in most cases. A number of pests including beetles, flies, worms, and nematodes can damage carrots when they are grown in the ground. In containers indoors, carrot plants should be free from pests. If care is taken not to water them too often, they should be free from fungi or other diseases common to carrot plants.

One of the fun things about growing carrots at home is the variety of interesting carrots you can try, virtually none of which are available in grocery stores. These carrot varieties include a number of different flavors, colors, and sizes. Tiny, round carrots make a fun snack for kids, and larger carrots that come in white, yellow, red, and even purple are also fun to try.

Cucumbers

Botanical name: *Cucumis sativus*

Common name: Cucumber

Family name: *Cucurbitaceae*

Origin: India

Light: Full sun

Size and growth: Fast-growing vines, up to 6' long

Minimum temperature: 60° Fahrenheit

Blooming season: Summer

Outside hardiness zone: 2-11

Best time to prune: Prune any dead growth

Pests or diseases to watch for: Cucumber beetles, squash vine borer, fungi

Fertilizer: High-nitrogen fertilizer, peat moss, compost, manure

Unique characteristics/growing tips: Long cucumber vines need significant space, and the cucumbers might be too heavy to grow the plant on a trellis.

Description:

Cucumbers are such hardy plants and produce so many vegetables that they remain one of the most popular plants for gardeners who want to grow edible plants. Like many vegetables, cucumbers come in a number of interesting varieties, many of which are not available in most grocery stores. These include round, yellow, and miniature varieties.

Cucumber plants require full sun and plenty of water. As long as they get these two things, they are hardy plants that will produce many cucumbers throughout the growing season. Although the plants are some of the hardiest of the garden vegetables, they have their share of pests if kept outdoors. Common pests, such as the beetle, can destroy whole vines if they are allowed to infest the plant.

The soil should contain some compost or peat moss to give it some of the nutrients the plants will need. Cucumber plants transplant well, so you can start the seeds in seed flats and transplant the young plants into larger pots if you desire. Young cucumber plants are also available at any nursery as well as most mass merchandise and home improvement stores. These young plants can be transplanted directly into a large container at least 12 inches wide. A larger container will allow for more growth and will give you a better yield of cucumbers.

Keep your cucumber plants in full sun. If you are growing them indoors, give them Southern exposures and make sure they are receiving as many hours of sunlight as possible each day. At least six to eight hours of sunlight are necessary for maintaining healthy cucumber plants.

Growing cucumbers in containers offers you the opportunity to keep the plants and their vegetables away from the ground. This can protect the plants from many of the worms that commonly infest cucumber plants. It also keeps the leaves and stems off the ground, which can prevent fungal infections. Because these plants need moist soil, constant contact with the soil can lead to plant diseases for leaves and stems. Trellising the vines is another option, as it keeps the vines growing vertically and away from the moist soil.

Cucumbers themselves are heavy and might not grow as well when the plant is vertically trellised. To assist the vegetables, tie them to the stake or trellis as they grow. This takes some of the weight of the vegetables off the plant and gives the cucumbers the support of the trellis or stake instead. As long as the temperature outside is at least 60 degrees, the containers can be kept outside. If you live in an area that is sunny and warm, keeping the plant outdoors might be the best area for cucumbers to grow.

A cucumber bush can reach about 4 feet in height and is often the best choice for container gardens. There are also dwarf varieties of cucumber bushes that reach about 2 feet in height. A cucumber vine, on the other hand, can reach 9 feet in length, making it difficult to grow indoors.

When you see any dead leaves, stems, or fruit, cut them off immediately to ensure the plant will not expend any energy on those areas. This is the only pruning cucumber plants really need. When the cucumbers are dark green, pick them by either twisting them away from their stem or by cutting them off. Some specialty cucumbers come in other colors, such as yellow. These will each have their own signs of ripeness, but they will be removed from the vine in the same way.

Garlic

Botanical name: *Allium sativum*

Common name: Garlic

Family name: *Alliaceae*

Origin: Asia

Light: Full sun to partial shade

Size and growth: As tall as 2' in height

Minimum temperature: 32° Fahrenheit

Blooming season: Late summer

Outside hardiness zone: 3-9

Best time to prune: No pruning is necessary

Pests or diseases to watch for: Maggots

Fertilizer: Organic fertilizer in spring and fall

Unique characteristics/growing tips: Each garlic clove will produce one garlic plant. The cloves contain a natural pesticide that can repel biting insects from the plant.

Description:

Like other edible plants, far more varieties of garlic exist than a regular grocery store can handle. In addition to the standard white garlic varieties, you can grow purple varieties, elephant garlic, and many others. Some have stronger tastes than others. Although larger in size than most varieties, elephant garlic has a milder taste. Elephant garlic is more accurately classified as an onion, but because it looks and tastes like garlic, it is often grown and used as a garlic variety.

Although garlic is a treat for maggots when grown in the ground, it has few other predators. It is resistant to most pests and diseases and is a resilient plant. Fall-planted garlic actually needs to be exposed to cold temperatures to begin the germination process.

Garlic prefers to have plenty of organic materials in its soil. Compost and peat moss can provide this environment, but manure is one of the best fertilizers for garlic plants. They should be fertilized in the fall and spring.

A garlic root is a bulb, and within that bulb are several cloves. Before planting garlic, open the bulb and remove the cloves. The largest clove from the bulb is generally the best one to plant, but all of them can be planted. Each clove should be planted about 2 inches beneath the surface of the soil with the "pointy" end of the clove pointed upward. Each clove should take root and grow into its own garlic plant. Water the plant regularly and keep the soil very lightly moist. It should never become waterlogged, and the soil should not dry out completely in between waterings.

Place garlic plants or cloves at least 6 inches apart to give the bulbs plenty of space to develop. If you are planting elephant garlic, increase the space to 10 inches. You can purchase garlic bulbs at local nurseries. They are generally sold in the fall so they can be planted right away. The plant should be planted into soil before there has been a freeze outdoors. To get the plant to grow in the spring, put the container outdoors for the winter or in a freezer to stimulate the natural germination process.

The garlic plant will begin growing in the spring, and be ready to harvest in the late spring to early summer, depending on the local climate. The plant should get full sunlight, but it will tolerate partial shade in most cases. The container should be at least 6 inches deep to accommodate a garlic plant. Although the bulb itself might be small, some varieties of garlic will grow to about 2 feet in height above the soil. The long, thin plant tends to bend over as it grows. If you are growing your garlic indoors, you might want to tie the plant to a stake to keep it out of the way.

When the foliage starts to turn yellow, the garlic is almost mature enough to harvest. Wait until about three-fourths of the foliage has turned yellow before harvesting the bulbs.

Lettuce and salad greens

Botanical name: *Lactuca sativa*

Common name: Lettuce

Family name: *Asteraceae*

Origin: The Mediterranean

Light: Full sun to light shade

Size and growth: Fast-growing, about 12" in height

Minimum temperature: 60° Fahrenheit

Blooming season: Late summer to fall

Outside hardiness zone: 6-11

Best time to prune: Pruning not necessary

Pests or diseases to watch for: Rabbits, caterpillars, slugs

Fertilizer: 10-10-10 fertilizer

Unique characteristics/growing tips: Shallow roots make it perfect for containers.

Description:

Lettuce is one of the most useful and versatile of all the vegetables grown at home. It can be used in main courses, side dishes, snacks, and more. It complements Italian, Mexican, American, French, and just about every other type of cuisine. Lettuce is eaten raw and can be kept in the refrigerator for a few weeks. With little to no preparation needed, lettuce is the ultimate convenience food.

Lettuce has shallow roots, making it a perfect container vegetable. A plant pot no more than 6 to 9 inches in depth is a good size for a lettuce plant. Lettuce also can be combined with a number of other salad greens for an interesting meal. Mustard greens, cucumbers, radishes, beets, and spinach are all commonly used together in salads. All of these items can be grown in containers. Because lettuce is a compact plant with shallow roots, you can grow it in the same container as other salad greens to create a salad garden.

Some seed companies sell salad green mixes that contain seeds for several salad green varieties together. These mixes are planted together so the plants all grow together, which creates a convenient garden that can be harvested at about the same time and used to make creative salads.

Lettuce does require full sunlight, but if the weather is too warm, it may need to be shaded from the sun. It prefers cool, sunny areas with temperatures of approximately 70 degrees, so it is a good crop for the late summer or the fall, depending on your local climate. If you have hot, sunny days that can damage your lettuce, simply remove the container from the mid-day sun to prevent overheating the plant. Outdoors, some gardeners place a screen or covering over the plant on those days to prevent the plant from getting too hot. High temperatures not only harm the plant, they can also change the taste of the lettuce.

When preparing the soil for growing lettuce, add some compost, manure, or a light dose of 10-10-10 fertilizer to the soil. Once the lettuce is planted, the soil should be kept moderately moist. The soil should not dry out between waterings, but keeping it waterlogged can lead to fungal infections and root rot. Make sure that the container has plenty of drainage, and always check the moisture level of the soil before watering to prevent over-watering. If the soil does dry out between waterings, the flavor of the leaves can change to a more bitter flavor.

Lettuce can be started in seed trays and transplanted into larger containers. The seedlings should be about one month old before they are transplanted. Most lettuce varieties will be mature within 60 to 110 days after sprouting, depending on the variety. The maturation times of other salad greens vary with the specific variety.

Leafy greens like lettuce and other salad greens are extremely susceptible to absorbing pesticides. Growing lettuce and other leafy greens at home is often done to ensure there are no pesticides in those plants. If you grow lettuce and other leafy greens at home, avoid any type of pesticide use.

There are many varieties of lettuce that can be grown at home. Although iceberg and Romaine are most commonly consumed in the United States, many other varieties will grow in containers. These can add some varieties to salads and might encourage you and your family to eat more salads. Butterhead lettuce has a sweet flavor and a soft, buttery texture. Crisphead lettuce has a sweet flavor and a crispy texture. Stem lettuce has a large seedstalk that is cooked and used in many Asian dishes.

Onions

Botanical name: *Allium cepa*

Common name: Garden onion

Family name: *Alliaceae*

Origin: Asia, the Mediterranean

Light: Full sun, partial shade

Size and growth: Above-ground and root size vary by variety

Minimum temperature: 20° Fahrenheit

Blooming season: Summer

Outside hardiness zone: 3-10

Best time to prune: No pruning is necessary

Pests or diseases to watch for: Onion maggots, rot

Fertilizer: 10-20-10 fertilizer

Unique characteristics/growing tips: Onions are hardy in cold weather and take up little space.

Description:

Onions are a staple in many households because of the variety of dishes that call for them. Everything from salad to salsa uses onions as flavoring, and the bulb is also nutritious. Many types of onions exist for you to choose from when growing the vegetable at home, including onions of different sizes, shapes, colors, and flavors.

Onions are ideal for container gardening because they do not take up much space. A large onion may be only 4 to 5 inches in diameter, meaning each onion plant only needs a small pot. If you want to grow several onion plants, choose a larger planter and place the onions about 6 inches apart.

Onions can be grown from seeds or transplanted seedlings. It is often easiest to grow them from young plants. If you choose to purchase plants, look for plants growing in biodegradable pots to disturb the bulb as little as possible. The neck of the onion bulb should be protruding slightly from your potting soil when you replant the bulb. The soil does not have to be deep to grow onions; a pot that is 6 inches deep is usually deep enough for an onion plant.

Onions needs some direct sunlight, but full sun during the hottest months can burn the plants. If you grow them during the summer months or live in a very hot climate, give onion plants partial shade or dappled sunlight to keep the plants from burning. Onions are cold-hardy and most varieties will not be killed by frost or even by a light freeze.

You might not need to add any fertilizer to your potting soil beyond simple compost or peat moss. However, if you do have trouble getting onions to grow, try adding a 10-20-10 fertilizer to the soil sparingly.

Onions grown in the ground are susceptible to a number of maggots and other pests. Onion bulbs grow under the soil, making root rot a problem. To avoid any rot, keep the soil slightly moist, but avoid over-watering. The drainage needs to be excellent to provide water regularly and ensure it is not collecting inside the container.

If you see any gray spots around the neck of the bulb, this is fungal growth. A white, fluffy growth at the bottom of the onion bulb is another type of fungal growth. In both cases, little can be done to control the growth of fungi. Cutting away the infected part of the plant will stop it from spreading, but it might also kill the plant. If there are multiple plants in the same pot that have fungal infections, all of the plants in the container may not be salvageable. Getting rid of the plants and thoroughly washing the container before using it again can help to keep the fungi from spreading to other plants.

Onions can take a long time to mature, which prompts many gardeners to plant them at staggered times of the year to provide a more steady supply of onions. There are two distinct growing seasons for onions — spring planting harvested in the late summer and fall planting harvested the following year.

When the plant's foliage begins to turn yellow, the bulbs are ready to harvest. Once onions are harvested, they can stay good for as long as six months. Keep them in the dark to prevent the bulbs from sprouting foliage.

Peas

Botanical name: *Pisum sativum*

Common name: Pea, sweet pea, field pea

Family name: *Fabaceae*

Origin: The Mediterranean, Asia

Light: Full sun to partial shade

Size and growth: 2-6' tall

Minimum temperature: 35° Fahrenheit

Blooming season: Spring, summer

Outside hardiness zone: 4-9

Best time to prune: Pruning is not necessary

Pests or diseases to watch for: Root rot, slugs

Fertilizer: Bone meal, manure

Unique characteristics/growing tips: Peas grow on tall vines and have large root systems.

Description:

Peas are a small, round member of the bean family. They grow in long pods, and each pod contains several peas. Pea plants are annuals; they grow and produce peas within one year. Pea-plant vines can be trained to grow on trellises, tall stakes, gazebos, and poles. This can make it more convenient to grow the plants indoors in containers. However, these plants have large root balls and need a deep container. A 5-gallon bucket with holes drilled in the bottom is a good container for a pea plant. Some dwarf pea varieties grow to only about 2 feet in height and take up less space.

Peas grow well from seeds, or you might decide to get a jump-start with a young plant from a nursery. If you are planting from seeds, plant them approximately 1 to 2 inches apart and thin out the plants once they have sprouted. Take the strongest plants and give each its own container. If you have a very large planter, you can place two pea plants together, but those plants will not have as much air circulation as a pea plant grown in its own pot. After planting seeds, you can expect the plant to mature within approximately 70 days.

When the vines begin to grow, use a tall stake or a trellis to support the plant. A 4-foot stake is tall enough to support most pea plant varieties. When fertilizing, bone meal or manure can be used. Some gardeners add eggshells to their pea plant soil instead of other fertilizers to add nutrients to the soil.

Pea plants are hardy and rarely succumb to disease if their moisture level is proper. The leaves and stems can be susceptible to fungal infections if they are allowed to droop over the soil. Tying the vines to a stake or trellis will keep the leaves away from the moist soil, which reduces the chance of fungi.

Pea plants need plenty of water, with water given every day and the soil kept moist. However, too much water kept on the roots can cause root rot, the biggest killer of pea plants. To avoid root rot, make sure the plant container is draining and no moisture is collecting in the soil. If the soil is already moist, do not add more water.

Pea plants need full sun in most areas. If you live in a hot, sunny climate, the pea plants might fare better in partial shade. Add some manure, bone meal, or crushed eggshells into the potting soil before planting.

If you are growing peas outdoors, slugs and insects that bore holes, such as beetles, can cause damage to the plants and the pods. The container in which peas are grown can act as a barrier between these insects and the plants, which cuts down on the number of insects that discover your pea plant. If you do find insects on your plant, cut away the area that is infested. Generally, a boring insect will only bore inside a pea pod, so it is easy to simply dispose of the pod to end the infestation.

Peas are not only hardy, they are also fun to harvest and can be eaten raw, right off the vine. Kids particularly like harvesting peas, picking the pea pods off the vines, and opening them to see the peas inside.

Potatoes

Botanical name: *Solanum tuberosum*

Common name: Potato

Family name: *Solanaceae*

Origin: South America

Light: Full sun

Size and growth: 2-4' in height

Minimum temperature: 45° Fahrenheit

Blooming season: Fall

Outside hardiness zone: 3-11

Best time to prune: No pruning is necessary

Pests or diseases to watch for: Beetles, aphids, wireworms, slugs, fungi

Fertilizer: Compost, peat moss

Unique characteristics/growing tips: Seek out disease-free seed potatoes.

Description:

There are more than 1,000 types of potatoes, few of which are ever available commercially. When you grow your own potatoes, you can experiment with different flavors and textures. Fresh potatoes are said to have a better taste than the potatoes available in stores.

Potato plants tend to become large quickly, and they can be difficult to grow in containers. You should place container potatoes either outdoors or in a large sunroom. Outdoors, potatoes can be grown inside a stack of tires, inside a large planter, or inside a potato bin. A potato bin is a large wooden bin that can be placed indoors or outdoors. Some people use a large trash can and drill holes in the bottom for drainage.

Once you have chosen your container, fill it about 5 inches deep with potting soil and compost or peat moss. Plant seed potatoes into the soil. Seed potatoes have at least two eyes and have sprouted. For the best results, purchase seed potatoes certified as disease-free potatoes. The potatoes sold in grocery stores can be harboring fungi or other diseases that make it impossible to grow a good potato crop. In addition, commercially grown potatoes might have been treated to keep them from sprouting. This treatment keeps them on the shelf longer, but it makes it difficult for the potato to grow any shoots.

The seed potato should have between one and three shoots. If it has any more, cut the portion with the additional shoots away and plant the rest. In a large container, you can plant four or five seed potatoes. They should be spaced about 12 inches apart. Cover the potatoes completely, including the shoots, with 1 inch of soil covering the tallest shoot. As the potato plant grows, continue adding soil and compost or peat moss to the container. Only a few inches of the potato shoot should be allowed to stay above the soil. Once the shoots become leafy, stop adding soil and organic materials. The plants will grow several feet tall, with the final height dependant on the variety.

Keep the soil slightly moist, but too much moisture can lead to fungal growth. Potato blight, famous for causing the Irish Potato Famine, can still cause damage to potato crops, and yours can be affected. If any of the foliage turns black, cut away the foliage and seal it in a plastic bag before discarding it or burn the affected foliage to keep it from spreading. If the blackened foliage does not comprise a significant portion of the plant, the plant can still thrive and will keep growing potatoes.

Potatoes grown in containers will be safer from predators, and they are easier to keep free of the fungal infections that can quickly kill potato plants. A container can keep the plants from slugs, which are a major cause of potato damage. Containers might also keep rodents from digging up the potatoes.

Another problem is the Colorado potato beetle. Despite its name, it can be found in most of North America and much of Europe. This beetle is notorious for destroying potato plants, and it is resistant to many common pesticides. These beetles spend the winter under the soil and attack new potatoes when they emerge from dormancy. Growing potatoes in containers can help to keep the plants away from this threat.

When the vines begin to die, the potatoes are ready to be harvested. Some potato bins are made with a handy opening on the side to allow you to pull out the potatoes. In other cases, dig them out, making sure to get all of the potatoes. There is no way to determine how many potatoes are growing in your container until they are harvested.

Spinach

Botanical name: *Spinacia oleracea*
Common name: Spinach
Family name: *Amaranthaceae*
Origin: Asia
Light: Full sun to partial shade
Size and growth: About 1' in height
Minimum temperature: 35° Fahrenheit
Blooming season: Spring or fall
Outside hardiness zone: 7-11
Best time to prune: Pruning is not necessary

Pests or diseases to watch for: Rabbits, rot, fungi, caterpillars
Fertilizer: Use a balanced organic fertilizer or fish emulsion every two weeks
Unique characteristics/growing tips: Inspect spinach plants regularly for insects.

Description:

Spinach is one of the most nutrient-dense foods, and it is also particularly susceptible to absorbing pesticides. This makes it a perfect vegetable to grow at home where you can ensure it does not come into contact with these chemicals. And, because spinach likes cooler weather and shorter days, you can have two spinach seasons: one in the spring and one in the fall.

Spinach plants are compact and require little growing room. Although the roots are shallow, spinach plants need a container at least 12 inches wide to accommodate the above-soil portion of the plant. Spinach will grow quickly, requiring cool temperatures and plenty of sunlight. If you keep your containers outdoors, full sunlight will work best during the spring and fall. In the summer, spinach will require some shade to avoid overheating. If you keep the container outdoors, consider spreading a 1-inch layer of mulch over the soil to help keep it moist.

Spinach requires moist soil conditions to thrive, but this moisture can lead to fungal growth as well as mold. Spinach needs a container with excellent drainage to avoid mold and fungal infections. The plants also need adequate air circulation. Place your spinach container so it has several inches of open space on all sides. If you keep your spinach pot outdoors, place it on a table or other high surface to keep rabbits and other animals away from it.

Spinach can be transplanted, but it prefers not to move. To avoid stunting growth or risking your plant, sow seeds directly into a container large enough to handle the plant's adult size.

When growing spinach plants from seed, plant a few seeds in the center of the container and thin out the seedlings a few weeks after they sprout. Keep only the strongest seedling in the container unless you are planting in a pot large enough to accommodate more than one. Spinach plants need about 6 inches of space between them.

Fish emulsion is a favorite fertilizer among spinach growers, but a balanced fertilizer such as 15-15-15 is a good alternative. Spinach plants grow quickly, and they should be fertilized every two weeks to help them continue the intake of nutrients. Without fertilizer, spinach can lose some of the dark color in its leaves, which signals a loss of nutrients.

Squash

Botanical name: *Cucurbita*
Common name: Squash, summer squash, winter squash
Family name: *Cucurbitaceae*
Origin: North and South America
Light: Full sun
Size and growth: Varies by variety
Minimum temperature: 60° Fahrenheit
Blooming season: Summer through fall
Outside hardiness zone: 3-10
Best time to prune: Pruning is not necessary
Pests or diseases to watch for: Beetles, squash bugs, powdery mildew
Fertilizer: Compost
Unique characteristics/growing tips: There are hundreds of varieties of these plants.

Description:

When most people think of squash, they picture the squash commonly called yellow squash. However, the term squash actually refers to an enormous and diverse group of vegetables including pumpkins, gourds, crookneck squash, and zucchini. When you grow squash, you can choose between everything from yellow crookneck squash to large, blue pumpkins. You can choose squashes of various sizes, from tiny, round ball squash to enormous gourds. Squash takes many shapes, including small, scalloped plants shaped like pies to elongated, skinny plants.

Summer squash and winter squash are popular terms to classify squash varieties, but these terms do not refer to when the vegetables actually grow.

 The terms describe how long it takes each type to ripen. Summer squash is harvested when the plant is still immature and the squash still tender. Winter squash is harvested when the squash is tough and has a thick rind.

Summer squashes, which include the familiar zucchini and yellow crookneck squash, have softer skins than winter squashes. These varieties are generally used for cooking because they have softer flesh. Summer squashes can have vines 3 feet in length or much longer, depending on the variety. Although these can be grown in containers indoors or out, most types need a support system that will hold the vines. Large or heavy vegetables might also need to be supported.

Pumpkins and other large squashes are impractical for growing in containers. Winter squashes have thick, tough skins and are harvested when they have fully matured. These varieties can have vines 25 feet in length, making them an impractical choice for most container gardeners. Smaller, bush-like varieties of squash are more suited for growing in containers.

Depending on the variety, squash seeds should be sown between the top layer of soil and an inch deep. All squash prefer warm weather and should be planted after the last frost has passed. When starting squash, add some compost to the potting soil, if possible. If you do not have compost, a high-nitrogen fertilizer can also be used.

Squash plants need plenty of water, but they are susceptible to molds and fungi. Check the water level carefully each day and avoid over-watering. The squash might need to be watered every day while bearing fruit. Summer squash varieties mature in about 50 days. Winter squash varieties can take as long as 110 days.

Although squash is not considered a hardy plant, it grows well and easily when it is given the right amount of water and sunlight. The plants

These ball squash seedlings are grown indoors in containers. Picture by Lizz Shepherd

produce many squash and continue producing for weeks, if not longer. If your squash plants are outdoors, inspect the undersides of the leaves regularly for squash bugs. These are tiny black bugs that attack squash leaves and lay red eggs on the leaves' undersides. If a leaf is infested with squash bugs, cut it off and dispose of the leaf far from away your plants.

Zucchini

Botanical name: *Cucurbita*
Common name: Zucchini, courgette
Family name: *Cucurbita pepo*
Origin: Italy
Light: Full sunlight
Size and growth: 5' in height
Minimum temperature: 65° Fahrenheit

Blooming season: Summer

Outside hardiness zone: All North American zones

Best time to prune: Fall

Pests or diseases to watch for: Aphids, spider mites, cucumber beetles, powdery mildew

Fertilizer: Organic fertilizer

Unique characteristics/growing tips: Zucchinis are rapid, liberal producers in rich soils.

Description:

Zucchini is a summer squash. Like other summer squashes, it has a short maturation time, about 40 to 50 days, depending on the variety. A standard zucchini plant will grow to about 5 feet in height, so it is difficult to grow them indoors. The full-size variety can be grown in containers on patios or in greenhouses if space is at a premium. A 5-gallon bucket, the minimum size needed to grow this plant, can be used as a planter for zucchini if you drill holes in the bottom to allow for drainage. However, miniature zucchini varieties can be grown in less space.

Spacemiser zucchini grows to about 18 to 24 inches in height and is perfect for indoor gardens. This plant might be small, but only the plant itself is a dwarf. The zucchini it produces is the same size as a standard zucchini plant. Another dwarf variety, eight ball, reaches about 12 to 18 inches in height, a good size for even the smallest indoor spaces. Eight ball does produce miniature zucchini, which are spherical in shape.

Although dwarf varieties will produce a smaller quantity of zucchini, a standard-size plant will be extremely productive if it is grown with the right amount of sunlight and fertilizer. Fertilizing with an organic fertilizer, such as compost or manure, when you plant can help keep the soil rich enough for it to produce well. If you are watering your plant daily and it starts to wilt or stops producing during the summer, it might need a larger container. When you water your plant, direct the water to the soil rather than to the leaves or stems. Wet leaves can cause mildew infections.

If zucchinis fall off the plant before it is mature, the plant is not getting enough water. Flowers that fall off without producing fruit are simply the male, non-producing flowers.

Check both sides of the leaves when watering to make sure the plant is not infested with pests. Spider mites will appear as tiny dots on the undersides of the leaves, or you might notice thin webs around the plant. Aphids will appear as tiny white dots anywhere on the plant. If grown indoors, cucumber beetles will likely not be a problem for your zucchini. If you do find a beetle on your plant, simply pick it off and check for others. If you discover aphids or spider mites, use an insecticidal soap to kill them or a damp cloth to wipe them away.

Common Mistakes to Avoid when Growing Vegetables

Most vegetable varieties require full sunlight in order to thrive and produce. If you are growing them indoors, think about the placement of your containers in terms of hours of sunlight per day instead of where it looks best or where it will fit best in terms of size. Full sunlight involves at least six hours of direct sunlight each day. A South-facing window will provide the most sunlight exposure.

Avoid adding outdoor soil to your containers. Over time, the soil inside a container can settle or become compacted in areas. Always add more potting soil or some organic fertilizer if indicated to the container instead of adding outdoor soil. The soil outdoors can introduce harmful bacteria, weed seeds, and other undesirable elements to your container.

Always check the leaves of your vegetable plants when you water them each day. Any mildew or other infections should be dealt with quickly before it spreads to other plants. If you see white or brown speckles on a leaf, the plant might be infected with mildew. Cut off the affected area, and check the surrounding leaves and stems. A badly infected plant should be removed from your indoor garden before it takes down the rest of your plants.

Make sure the container has drainage holes appropriate for the container size and that you protect indoor surfaces from the drainage. Some larger vegetable plants, such as zucchini, require large pots, and those pots will destroy flooring if you do not provide adequate protection from the drainage. A large pot that has drainage holes on the bottom might not be able to drain well if you place the pot onto a hard surface to hold the drainage. If the pot is to be kept indoors and placed onto a hard surface such as a larger pot or onto plastic sheeting, the pot must have holes at the point where the sides and bottom meet. If your pot does not have them, use a drill or a sharp knife to create them. Outdoors, downward-facing holes will work if the container will be placed on a stand, the ground, or a porous surface such as concrete.

If your vegetable plants are kept outdoors, you might need to water them more than once a day. Although potting soil is formulated to hold moisture, most vegetables require liberal watering during the summer months. This means watering them twice per day and perhaps even three times if you live in a hot, sunny climate. With proper drainage in the container, it would be hard to over-water outdoor vegetable plants, but when you do water, make sure to water the soil instead of the plant in order to avoid several preventable plant diseases.

Make sure you understand the size of the plant before you take on indoor vegetable gardening. Vegetable plants grow rapidly, and if the plant is not a dwarf variety, it might be too large for your indoor garden. Some, such as many varieties of squash, cucumbers, and peas, require trellising, which can be difficult to do indoors. A large or climbing variety might be best grown on a deck or patio.

CASE STUDY: USING CONTAINERS IN SMALL SPACES

Sandi Valentine
Valentine Content Creation, owner
valentinecontentcreation@gmail.com
www.valentinecontentcreation.com
Phone: (304) 616-9175

I spent several years living in an urban apartment with no garden space. I grew vegetables and herbs on my porch and sidewalk each year. In addition, I currently write for GardenGuides.com on the topics of urban homesteading, container gardening, and home composting.

Containers offer a controlled soil environment for plants, which allows the gardener to regulate the alkalinity of the soil, add compost as necessary, and meet the needs of individual plants. Containers also work well for those who have limited gardening space or who want to grow an indoor garden due to climate or space concerns.

People might choose to grow food indoors to supplement their purchases from farmers' markets and grocery stores or because they enjoy beautifying their space. Apartment dwellers and those who live in areas without access to outdoor gardening space might find a container garden especially enjoyable.

Irrigation and pest control can become issues with an indoor container garden; however, both issues can usually be managed successfully. For example, household greywater can be re-used to water indoor plants.

The number of plants generally manageable to house indoors depends greatly on the space each individual has available. Plants can be grown in outdoor containers on a rooftop or balcony and can make quite an extensive garden, or they can be grown indoors on a windowsill.

Herbs, such as basil and rosemary, generally grow quite well indoors. Depending on the light source available, vegetables, fruits, and flowers can also be grown indoors.

It is difficult to grow fruit trees indoors, as well as any plant that needs a large amount of sunlight, such as a tomato. However, these plants might grow well in an outdoor container garden. If you have a large enough container and space available, you can grow nearly anything.

As the economy worsens, people are more interested in being self sufficient and saving money whenever possible. By growing their own food, they can enjoy organic produce at a fraction of the cost of purchasing the same items at the grocery store.

You can save money and enjoy a rewarding hobby when you grow your own food. In addition, you can choose to grow foods that are organic, and limit your family's consumption of genetically modified (GMO) foods. If you purchase heirloom seeds, you can save seeds from year to year and reduce the cost of your garden drastically.

Chapter 9

GROWING FRUITS IN CONTAINERS

L ike herbs and vegetables, fruit can be grown in indoor and outdoor containers. Although some fruit trees, such as apples, are too large to be grown indoors, large outdoor planters can grow virtually any type of fruit. Many fruit varieties grow on small trees or bushes that take up little space. There are many dwarf varieties that take up even less space. A full-size lime tree might grow to 15 feet in height, but there are dwarf varieties that reach only 3 to 5 feet in height.

Lemon, orange, peach, and apple trees can be grown outdoors in large wooden planters. Strawberries, raspberries, dwarf pomegranates, and some blueberry varieties can be grown in smaller containers indoors or out. Grapes and currants can be grown indoors or out with the proper trellising.

Other than outdoor planters, there are ways to plant large fruit-bearing plants. Cutting an old barrel in half will give you two large planters. A wooden shipping container can also be used. Old plastic milk crates covered in mesh can be used to hold a mid-sized fruit plant.

Drainage is important for growing any plant in a container, but fruit plants particularly need a lot of drainage attention. Too little drainage will quickly kill a fruit plant. Some gardeners place gravel in the bottom of their fruit plant containers to ensure the plants' roots will not sit in moisture.

In general, fruit plants require full sunlight in order to produce fruit. Stunted sunlight exposure means stunted plants and stunted fruit size and abundance. Some fruit plants will tolerate partial shade, some require full sunlight, and some need to be protected from the sun during the hottest part of the day.

Can You Really Grow Fruits in Containers?

Growing larger fruit plants, such as large fruit trees, can be difficult in containers, but it is possible. Some fruit trees, such as peach trees, require frequent root pruning to keep the plants small enough to be contained by a planter. If you have a large outdoor space, you can grow fruit trees of virtually any variety.

Because fruit trees must be kept at a manageable size when they are grown in containers, they will not produce as much fruit as a tree grown in the ground. However, container-grown fruit trees often produce fruit one to two years earlier than fruit trees grown in the ground.

To grow fruit, few supplies are needed other than solid containers, potting soil, water, and sunlight. If you live in an area that typically receives little sunlight each year, such as the Pacific Northwest, you may need a UV grow lamp to grow fruit.

Why Grow Your Own Fruit?

Fruits are nutritious foods that are a part of a healthy daily diet. They have natural sugars that make them ideal for desserts, snacks, and a light meal. Fruits are easy to grow, and they can be preserved and enjoyed for years to come. Many gardeners grow fruit to have seasonal, fresh fruit available during the growing season and to can the fruit to enjoy during the rest of the year.

Canning might sound old fashioned, but it is easy and inexpensive to do, and it can be a big help to a family's grocery budget. It is possible to can as much fruit as you grow and not worry about buying fruit through the fall, winter, and spring. Good quality produce is expensive, and it goes bad quickly, necessitating many trips to the grocery store to keep a home stocked while it is in season. During the growing season, you will never have to run to the store to replace the fruit you have run out of, which will save you time and money. Instead, you can simply pick fresh fruit from your own plants.

Fruits such as pears, peaches, apples, raspberries, and strawberries are known as the worst fruits for pesticide concentration. It is particularly important to eat organically grown versions of these fruits when possible. Organic fruit is even more expensive than the typical produce sold at grocery stores, but when you grow it from home, it is less expensive to grow it organically than it would be to cover it in pesticides and herbicides. With container plants, you do not need to apply herbicides, and many pesticides are unnecessary. By simply not applying pesticides, you can grow an abundance of organic fruit for far less money than a one-week supply of organic produce from the grocery store.

Ornamental Fruit

An ornamental fruit tree is one known for its attractive appearance. These are often planted purely for landscaping appeal because of their beautiful leaves, distinct flowers, or the colors the trees turn in the spring or fall. Many of these fruit trees produce edible fruit, so the trees are doubly enticing to grow. They brighten up porches and doorways and grow a useful, edible fruit.

Ornamental fruit varieties include pineapple plants as well as chokeberry, crabapple, pineapple, pear, apple, and lime trees. All of these can be grown in containers in either their standard or dwarf varieties.

Standard crabapple trees can grow to 20 feet in height, but smaller varieties, such as the 10-foot Sargent variety, will grow well in a planter. A key lime plant is a tiny lime tree that grows tiny fruit. These trees can be kept at about 5 feet and will produce fruit 1 to 2 inches in diameter. Many dwarf lemon and lime varieties exist that can be kept under 10 feet high and will produce plenty of fruit at that size.

Pineapple plants are perhaps one of the most popular ornamental fruit plants due to their unusual foliage and compact size. A pineapple plant grows to about 2 ½ to 5 feet in height and produces spiny leaves from a center rosette. It blooms with red or purple flowers.

A kumquat tree grows to about 8 to 15 feet in height, blooms with yellow flowers, and produces a fruit with a sweet, edible rind. It is also more cold-hardy than any other citrus tree with edible fruit and blooms later in the year than other citrus trees.

Some ornamental fruit trees, such as several varieties of pear trees, produce inedible fruit. The Bradford pear is a popular ornamental for its compact size, the enormous numbers of white flowers that bloom in the spring, and its red foliage in the fall, but the fruit is poisonous. If you have children, growing an indoor plant with an inedible fruit can be dangerous to those in the household.

A Complete List of Container-grown Fruits

Growing fruit in containers is often considered a little more challenging than growing vegetables. Although some fruits grow easily in containers and are not picky about soil conditions, such as a strawberries, others have specific soil pH requirements to keep the plant thriving and producing.

Blueberries

Botanical name: *Cyanococcus*

Common name: Blueberry

Family name: *Ericaceae*

Origin: Europe and North America

Light: Full sunlight

Size and growth: 1-5'

Minimum temperature: -10° Fahrenheit

Blooming season: Spring

Outside hardiness zone: 3-10

Best time to prune: Spring

Pests or diseases to watch for: Powdery mildew, fruit flies, leafrollers, aphids, blueberry maggots

Fertilizer: Sulphur

Unique characteristics/growing tips: Highbush, lowbush, and rabbiteye varieties vary widely in size. Blueberries need an acidic soil and should be fertilized monthly.

Description:

Blueberries require an acidic soil with a pH of about 4.0 to 5.5. Getting a soil pH kit from a gardening or home improvement store can help you keep track of the pH level in your blueberry container. To make the soil slightly more acidic, add a tablespoon of granulated sulphur to the potting soil before planting. Mix the sulphur into the soil well before planting.

The type of blueberry plant you choose will likely come down to your climate and how large you want your plants. Blueberry plants live for several years, so it might be two years or more before a young blueberry plant will produce fruit.

A rabbiteye blueberry plant is the largest and grows to approximately 15 feet in height. These generally need to be grown outdoors because of their height, but they can be grown in large outdoor containers such as 10-gallon planters. Rabbiteye blueberry varieties grow best with organic materials such as compost or peat moss added to the soil. About 2 percent of the soil should be organic materials. The top of the soil should be mulched to help hold moisture in the soil. These varieties grow to about 8 to 10 feet in width, but pruning can keep them a more manageable size for containers.

Highbush blueberry varieties grow to about 5 to 6 feet in height and are easier to manage in containers. They produce the type of blueberries that are commonly found in grocery stores. With highbush varieties, all of the flowers that bloom in the first year should be removed in order to help the plant establish itself and bloom better in subsequent years. Highbush blueberries need about 3 percent organic materials in the soil and should be mulched.

Lowbush blueberry plants grow to about 1 to 2 feet in height and produce blueberries in their second year. The flowers should be removed during the first year. This type can be grown in a 5-gallon bucket with drainage drilled along the bottom edge. Like other varieties, it should be mulched to keep the soil moist. Mulching with pine bark will add a little acidity to the soil. The pH level should stay between 4.0 and 5.6.

All blueberry varieties grow in clumps of canes that should be pruned every spring to allow the stronger canes to grow. Weak canes should be cut back to allow stronger canes more sunlight and aeration. This also allows them to become strong enough to support a large crop of blueberries. More aggressive pruning to remove the older canes will encourage new growth, which will produce a larger-sized berry.

If you are growing your blueberries outdoors, they should be covered with netting to prevent birds from feasting on the berries. Staking a net so that it remains several inches away from the plant will ensure birds cannot slip their beaks through the netting and sneak a meal of fresh blueberries. Although the soil should remain moist, getting too much water on the canes and leaves can result in mildew.

Raspberries

Botanical name: *Rebus idaeus*

Common name: Raspberry

Family name: *Rosaceae*

Origin: Europe

Light: Full sunlight, partial sunlight

Size and growth: 4-6' in height, 4-6' in width

Minimum temperature: 50° Fahrenheit

Blooming season: Spring, summer

Outside hardiness zone: 3-8

Best time to prune: Spring, summer

Pests or diseases to watch for: Root rot, gray mold, viruses, aphids, birds

Fertilizer: 5-10-5

Unique characteristics/growing tips: Raspberries should be pruned of any dead wood to keep the plant producing new growth.

Description:

Raspberries do well in cool climates and are not picky about their soil type. They need large pots to ensure plenty of room for their large root balls and require full sunlight. Containers should be at least 2 to 3 feet deep to allow the root ball enough depth. There are dozens of raspberry varieties, including red, black, yellow, and purple varieties.

A 10-10-10 fertilizer should be added once the plant is established in the container. They need to be watered daily, but make sure that the roots do not sit in too much water. Drainage is essential. Add mulch to the top of the soil to retain moisture. Like blueberries, raspberries grow in multiple canes that should be thinned to enable the stronger canes to thrive.

Raspberries will produce berries from spring through mid-summer, with some varieties baring fruit earlier than others. Summer-bearing and everbearing varieties are available, with each producing berries at different times of the year. The canes grow to about 4 to 5 feet in height.

Raspberry plants are extremely susceptible to mold and viruses spread by aphids. To keep your plant healthy, keep water away from the leaves and stems and check them often for aphids.

Blackberries

Botanical name: *Rebus fruticosus*

Common name: Blackberry

Family name: *Rosaceae*

Origin: South America

Light: Full sunlight

Size and growth: 3-0'

Minimum temperature: -20° Fahrenheit

Blooming season: Summer

Outside hardiness zone: 5-10

Best time to prune: Summer, fall

Pests or diseases to watch for: Mildew, birds, rabbits

Fertilizer: 10-10-10

Unique characteristics/growing tips: Erect blackberry plants are often easier to grow in containers.

Description:

Blackberries generally need full sunlight, but they will tolerate partial shade if they are given a few hours of direct sunlight each day. There are two main types of blackberries: erect and trailing. Each type has several cultivars available with a slightly different size, flavor, and fruit-baring abundance. Some have thorns and some were bred to be thornless.

Erect blackberry plants will grow into a self-sustaining bushy shape, but trailing blackberries generally need a trellis or other support to keep them erect. They can be trained to climb a fence, wrap around stakes, or grow around a porch railing.

Blackberry canes produce berries on a two-year cycle, with the fruit being produced in the second year. After the second year, a cane should be cut back to enable the growth of new, berry-producing canes.

Too much water will kill a blackberry plant within two to three days, so large drainage holes are necessary if you live in a rainy climate. In the absence of rain, blackberry plants should be watered every other day to avoid too much water. A 5-10-5 fertilizer in the spring will keep the potting soil rich enough for blackberry growth.

Blackberries are easy to pull away from the cane when they are ripe. If you have trouble pulling the berry away from the plant, the berry is not yet ripe. When the berries ripen, pick them every three to six days to prevent losing ripened berries. Like blueberries, staking a net around the plant will prevent birds from eating the ripe berries.

Gooseberries

Botanical name: *Ribes uva-crispa*

Common name: Gooseberry

Family name: *Grossulariaceae*

Origin: Europe, Asia, Africa

Light: Full sunlight, partial shade

Size and growth: 4-5'

Minimum temperature: -28° Fahrenheit

Blooming season: Spring

Outside hardiness zone: 3-8

Best time to prune: Summer

Pests or diseases to watch for: Aphids, spider mites, gooseberry sawfly, mildew

Fertilizer: Manure

Unique characteristics/growing tips: Gooseberry leaves can burn in hot climates when given full sunlight.

Description:

Gooseberries are long-lived berry bushes that can bear berries for 15 years or longer. The plant grows to about 3 to 5 feet in height. Like other berry bushes, the plant grows outward with numerous canes. These canes should be thinned to allow more sunlight and air circulation for the strongest canes. The center of the plant should be kept clear of canes to allow them to grow without becoming tangled. Tangled branches will not get enough air and can suffer from fungal infections due to too little air circulation. Each winter, cut away any dead canes and any growing across the center of the plant.

Gooseberry plants need full sunlight, and they should be fertilized with 10-10-10 or manure fertilizer in the spring. If you live in a hot climate, provide them with some shade during the hottest part of the day or keep the container in partial shade. Mulch the top of the soil with at least 2 inches of mulch to keep the soil moist and cool. Flowers should be removed during the first year to encourage new growth.

A gooseberry plant can be trained to grow in a tree-like structure by cutting away all of the lower buds on the canes; keep only the top four buds. This will give the plant "legs" and a more erect shape. This will also keep the foliage away from the soil and make a fungal or mildew infection less likely. Once a shoot becomes four years old, cut it away to make room for newer, more productive canes.

Citrus fruit

Botanical name: *Citrus sinenis*

Common name: Orange

Family name: *Rutaceae*

Origin: Southeast Asia

Light: Full sunlight

Size and growth: 5-30', dependent on variety

Minimum temperature: 50 Fahrenheit

Blooming season: Spring

Outside hardiness zone: 9-11

Best time to prune: Fall

Pests or diseases to watch for: Red spider mites, citrus borer, codling moth, aphids, mealy bugs, root rot

Fertilizer: High-acid fertilizer or fish emulsion

Unique characteristics/growing tips: Oranges need cooler temperatures in the winter in order to create the dormancy and growth cycle that produces fruit.

Description:

Standard-sized orange trees are simply too large to grow in containers, but many dwarf varieties grow well and grow specialty varieties of this popular citrus fruit. Dwarf orange trees can be as small as 2 to 3 feet in height and produce tiny, miniature oranges about 2 inches in diameter. The dwarf varieties grow smaller fruit, but their yield can be high if they are properly cared for.

A high-acid fertilizer or fish emulsion should be added to the soil once a month from spring through fall. Orange trees need to be watered regularly with enough water to allow the roots to be penetrated by the moisture. Allow the plant heavy drainage to avoid root rot. The soil should be kept moist at all times. If the tree is kept in an indoor container, mist the plant lightly to give it the high level of humidity it requires. When watering, keep the water away from the trunk.

Dwarf tangerines, a related plant, grow to a similar size and produce 2- to 4-inch fruits. Dwarf varieties of this tree can reach anywhere from 2 to 5 feet in height, depending on the variety. The dwarf tangelo tree, another related fruit tree, grows to about 12 feet high. Dwarf tangelo trees grow slowly and can live for years in a simple 5-gallon pot before needing a large outdoor planter.

Lemon

Botanical name: *C. limon*
Common name: Lemon
Family name: *Rutaceae*
Origin: Southeast Asia
Light: Full sunlight
Size and growth: 2-30'
Minimum temperature: 55° Fahrenheit
Blooming season: Spring and summer

Outside hardiness zone: 8-11

Best time to prune: After the fruit has been picked

Pests or diseases to watch for: Aphids, citrus borer, fungi, spider mites, citrus rust mites

Fertilizer: High-acid fertilizer

Unique characteristics/growing tips: If the temperature falls below 55° Fahrenheit, a lemon tree will fall into dormancy. Bring the container inside or protect the plant from the cold with heavy mulching and a tarp covering.

Description:

A standard-sized lemon tree can reach 30 feet in height and is not well suited for containers. Like oranges, however, there are many interesting dwarf and hybrid varieties that can be grown in a large pot or outdoor planter.

The Meyer lemon is a popular lemon variety for containers and indoor growers. This lemon variety is small in size, with a maximum height of approximately 4 feet, but it produces full-size lemons. Many people keep these as purely ornamental plants because of their dark leaves and white flowers. They are also less thorny than full-sized lemon trees, with small thorns that do not appear as often on the branches.

Any variety of lemon tree is extremely sensitive to the cold. They must be taken indoors if the temperature drops to the mid-50s or below. Lemon trees also need excessive sunlight. Getting six hours of sunlight per day is needed for most full-sunlight plants, but a lemon tree requires far more. Some experts suggest 12 hours of sunlight each day to keep lemon trees thriving. Using a UV lamp for indoor trees will help to supplement the amount of light they receive through a window.

Like orange trees, lemon trees crave humidity. The soil should stay moist at all times, and you should mist indoor lemon trees with a plant mister or a regular spray bottle that can produce a fine mist. Lemon trees generally need to be watered daily and misted approximately three times per week.

Like other citrus plants, Meyer lemon trees require their soil to be slightly acidic. Using an acidic fertilizer, such as one for rhododendrons, each spring will add some of this needed acidity to the soil.

To produce lemons, a lemon tree does need to be pollinated. If you keep your tree outdoors, the insects and the wind will do the job for you, but if your tree is indoors, you must pollinate it yourself. Do this by taking a small paintbrush and spreading the pollen within each flower around to the other parts of the flower.

Lime

Botanical name: *Citrus aurantifolius*

Common name: Lime

Family name: *Rutaceae*

Origin: Southeast Asia

Light: Full sunlight

Size and growth: 2-15', dependant on variety

Minimum temperature: 55° Fahrenheit

Blooming season: Spring

Outside hardiness zone: 9-11

Best time to prune: Winter

Pests or diseases to watch for: Sooty mold, root rot, leafminer, scale, aphids, spider mites

Fertilizer: Nitrogen-rich fertilizer

Unique characteristics/growing tips: Limes are picked and eaten before they ripen. They require acidic soil.

Description:

Like other citrus fruit trees, standard lime trees can be difficult to manage in containers. However, the standard-sized lime tree is smaller than the orange or lemon tree. At 15 feet tall and about 15 feet wide, it is possible to grow lime trees in large outdoor planters. However, many interesting dwarf varieties are easier to manage in containers and small enough to keep indoors.

The smallest dwarf lime tree varieties grow to about 2 feet in height. Other varieties will grow to 3, 5, or 8 feet in height. Dependent on the variety, these will grow either full-size limes or smaller, specialty limes. The key lime tree grows tiny, 1- to 2-inch fruit with a unique, tart flavor. The tree can be pruned to a height of about 3 to 5 feet and can be kept indoors.

All lime trees need full sunlight. If kept indoors, a lime tree should be given a south-facing window for the maximum sunlight exposure each day. In the winter, consider a UV lamp if you live in a less-sunny climate. Fertilize your tree in the spring and summer with a high-nitrogen fertilizer. Lime trees can also benefit from adding compost to the soil at a percentage of about 2 percent of the total potting soil. Water the tree each day and mist the entire plant three times a week. Like lemon trees, they will need hand-pollination if they are grown indoors.

Limes are actually yellow and resemble lemons when they are ripe. However, limes are generally picked while they are still green and eaten before they are allowed to ripen. This is part of what gives the familiar grocery store lime its green color and its sour taste. Limes are useful in fish recipes, pies, and drinks.

Inspect outdoor lime trees daily for pests. Citrus trees are highly susceptible to a large number of pests, such as aphids and glassy-winged sharpshooters, and they can sicken the tree if not removed. Look for small dots, round waxy spots, and thin webs on or around the leaves and stems. These are all signs of a pest infestation. Insecticidal soap can kill the pests, or you can simply remove infected areas of the tree.

Currants

Botanical name: *R. rubrum*

Common name: Currant

Family name: *Grossulariaceae*

Origin: Europe

Light: Shade to partial shade

Size and growth: 4-6' in height, 2-5' wide

Minimum temperature: -40° Fahrenheit

Blooming season: Spring

Outside hardiness zone: 3-8

Best time to prune: Winter

Pests or diseases to watch for: White pine blister rust, aphids, currant fruit fly

Fertilizer: 5-10-5 fertilizer

Unique characteristics/growing tips: Growing black currants is prohibited in some regions because of the threat white pine blister rust poses to other plants. Check your local regulations to find out whether you can legally grow them.

Description:

Currants are full of antioxidants and potassium, and they are often used in jellies or eaten alone as a nutritious snack. There are three primary types of currents: red, white, and black currants. Each type has its own unique flavor and color. They are sometimes grown as ornamental plants because of their compact size and striking berries. They are also heavy producers, with one plant producing as much as 10 pounds of berries in a single year.

Unlike many fruit plants, currants can be damaged by too much sunlight. In a hot, sunny climate, direct sunlight can burn the plant and stunt its

growth. Cool temperatures and some protection from the sun are best for healthy currants. Currants should not be kept outdoors in areas where the temperature reaches 85 degrees or higher. Currant plants need a slightly acidic soil pH of 5.5 to 7.0.

Red currants are perhaps the most popular type to grow because of their mild flavor and easy availability at nurseries and commercially at grocery stores. White currants are known for their sweet flavor, though seedlings can be difficult to find. Red and white currents both produce blue-green leaves that make these plants interesting ornamentals. Black currents are sweet and are high in vitamin C, with triple the amount of this antioxidant vitamin as in oranges.

All currant plants were banned in the United States for several decades, but now, most regions allow currant cultivation. Red and white currants are allowed in every region, but black currants are still restricted as possible disease carriers. Several black currant varieties have been cultivated to be free of white pine blister rust, a dangerous form of rust that has damaged some Northeastern forests. However, Maine, New Hampshire, and Massachusetts still have black currant bans in place. If you do grow black currants, look for a rust-resistant cultivar such as Consort.

Currants are not generally grown from seed, but they do transplant well from seedlings or cuttings. Compost or manure added to the potting soil will give them a rich bed in which to thrive. Give the plant a 5-10-5 fertilizer in the spring. A seaweed-rich fertilizer is also good for currants. Black currants need to be fertilized more often than other currant types and require an extra fertilization in the summer.

Before planting currant seedlings, cut them to about 6 to 10 inches above the soil. This will encourage new growth once the plant is established. About 2 inches of mulch should be added to the soil to keep in moisture. The mulch will also help keep the summer heat away from the roots, which need to be kept cool year round. Water the plant often to keep the soil slightly moist. Wood chips, straw, or grass clippings will work as mulch for a currant plant. Adding a few pine needles or a few pieces of pine bark into the mix will give the soil a little extra acidity.

The plant grows outward from a center structure, with canes that should be kept away from the center. With the center area open, all of the canes get better light and air distribution. The best number of canes for a healthy plant and good berry production is ten to 14. Cut out the smaller canes until you reach this amount. The remaining canes will be able to grow stronger and larger, which makes them better able to produce berries. The best-producing canes are ones about a year old. Once you harvest currents from a cane, cut that cane back to allow for the growth of new canes.

The container you use should be at least 3 feet wide by 2 to 3 feet deep. This will allow for plenty of room for an adult currant plant. The canes themselves should be trellised or staked to keep them upright.

Like other berries, currents are a favorite food for many bird species. Keep a net over outdoor currant plants in order to keep some for your own currant harvest. Aphids can also be a serious problem for currant plants. A large outdoor plant can be rid of aphids with a strong water stream directed at the infected areas. An insecticidal soap or a thorough removal of the infected leaves can also quell an aphid uprising.

The currant fruit fly looks like a smaller version of the common housefly, but it can do far more damage to a currant tree. The fly lays eggs onto young berries, which causes the destruction of the berries as the young hatchlings eat them. One way to tell an infected currant is an early ripening of a few berries. Those berries will reach their mature color faster and then fall off the cane. If this should occur, remove those berries from the container to prevent the rest of the plant from being infected with the young flies.

If you purchase a young seedling, it might not produce any berries until its second year. Once the berries turn their mature color, wait approximately two weeks before harvesting them to allow them to fully ripen.

Grapes

Botanical name: *Vitis*

Common name: Grapes

Family name: *Vitaceae*

Origin: Europe, Middle East

Light: Full sunlight

Size and growth: 4-10' tall, 6-12' wide

Minimum temperature: 20° Fahrenheit

Blooming season: Spring

Outside hardiness zone: 4-10

Best time to prune: Fall and spring

Pests or diseases to watch for: Red spider mite

Fertilizer: 16-16-8

Unique characteristics/growing tips: Grape vines need a sturdy trellis.

Description:

Grape plants can be grown in pots indoors or out, and each plant will produce grapes for years. There are dozens are varieties of grapes, each with its own unique color and taste. White, pink, yellow, red, green, and purple grapes have flavors that range from slightly bitter to sweet. A healthy plant can produce as much as 15 pounds of grapes in a year.

Fertilize grape plants in the early spring with a 16-16-8 fertilizer while keeping the fertilizer away from the trunk. Mix the fertilizer into the soil at least 6 inches away from the trunk in order to avoid damaging it.

Choosing a grape type can be a difficult decision because of the many varieties available and the many uses of each type. Table grapes refer to grape varieties eaten raw. Thompson seedless, flame, and Concord grapes are popularly grown as table grapes, which are the grapes most often found for sale in grocery stores. Table grapes are generally not used as raisins or for wine or grape juice production.

Each grape plant should be planted at least 8 feet apart and farther for some varieties, so if you are growing your grapes indoors, more than one grape plant is probably not feasible. Grape growing requires dedication to pruning and training the vines, and it does require patience. Depending on the variety and the age of the plant you buy, it might be as long as four years after you have planted your grapes before you first see the fruit appear on the vines.

Add a small amount of sand or gravel into your container to help with drainage. Grapes like moisture, but if they stay wet for too long, the roots can quickly die. They grow wild in sandy soil and need excellent drainage to prevent root rot, mildew, and fungal infections. During the first month after transplanting, water them often, adding enough water to the container to soak the roots.

Compost should be added to the soil in order to give the plant enough nutrients to keep the leaves healthy. If the leaves are a dark green color, they have enough nutrients to thrive. If they begin to lose color before they fall, they might need more compost.

A sturdy trellis is essential because each grape bunch will be large and heavy. Wooden stakes are generally not sturdy enough to support grape vines and the resulting fruit. During the first two years, the vines will need to be trained by hand to climb in the direction you desire. Some grape growers spiral them around wires or thin posts held between two sturdy vertical posts. A wooden trellis like the ones sold in home improvement stores will work as long as the base is sufficiently supported. An outdoor container can be placed in front of a trellis driven into the ground behind it. Indoors, a trellis can be nailed to the back of a wooden container.

Pruning grape plants keeps them from growing too large, and it keeps them producing more fruit and fewer branches and leaves. Pruned grape vines grow larger grapes, and they can be kept to a more convenient size for containers. Pruning should not be done during the growing season in the spring. Instead, wait until the plant has lost its leaves in the fall or prune it in the very early spring before any new growth appears. Cut the vines that grow out from the side. These vines produce few grapes and will divert the plant's energy. Keeping your vines pruned will also allow the plant to get more sunlight. This is particularly important if you are growing them indoors and need to maximize the available sunlight.

Like other berries, grapes will benefit from a net erected around the plant to keep the birds at bay. They also need to be protected from aphids and other pests. Adding ladybugs to the grapevine will take care of any aphids. If you see tiny bugs on the leaves or stems, you might have spider mites. Cut away the infected leaves and dispose of them far away from any of your other plants to prevent a re-infestation. Then, check the other leaves for mites.

If you grow your grape plant indoors, you might need to pollinate the flowers in order to get the plant to produce grapes. For an easier growing experience, look for self-pollinating cultivars. Muscadines, bluebell, beta, prairie star, valiant, and Frontenac are just a few of the self-pollinating cultivars available on the commercial market.

Indoors, you might decide to keep grape plants for their leaves or simply for their ornamental appearance. Grape leaves are used in traditional Middle Eastern, Greek, Asian, and Eastern European cooking. A grape vine pruned to a small size can provide attractive, dark-green foliage for an indoor container.

Cantaloupe

Botanical name: *Cucumis melo*

Common name: Cantaloupe

Family name: *Cucurbitaceae*

Origin: Egypt

Light: Full sunlight

Size and growth: 10' climbing vines

Minimum temperature: 70° Fahrenheit

Blooming season: Summer

Outside hardiness zone: 4-10

Best time to prune: As needed for size

Pests or diseases to watch for: Powdery mildew, aphids, squash bugs, beetles

Fertilizer: 10-10-10

Unique characteristics/growing tips: Miniature cantaloupes can be grown indoors, but full-size cantaloupes should be grown in outdoor containers.

Description:

Because cantaloupes grow on long vines, as long as 10 feet in length, need constant heat and sunlight, and grow large, heavy melons, they can be difficult and complicated to grow indoors. Outdoors the plant can be grown in a planter if the vines are allowed to trail across the ground or onto a short trellis. The fruit are so heavy, however, that the plant cannot be grown upright on a trellis or stakes. If you have the space outdoors, having a vine trail out of the container and across the ground is fine.

Dwarf cantaloupe varieties can be grown in containers indoors or used to make outdoor containers more manageable. Either type will need full sunlight most of the day and soil temperatures of at least 70 degrees. Miniature cantaloupe varieties will grow a fruit about the size of a baseball to the size of a softball, depending on the variety. The outer rind will have a different color and texture from traditional North American cantaloupes, but the inside will have a very similar flavor and color. A miniature cantaloupe will have a climbing vine that grows to about 4 feet in length.

Outdoor cantaloupes should be checked for beetles and other pests, while indoor plants will likely only be susceptible to aphids and mildew. Whether the plant is indoors or out, it should be watered every day. Outdoor plants in hot, sunny climates should be watered twice a day. Water the soil instead of the foliage to avoid powdery mildew. Watch for a white, powdery color on the leaves and remove any infected leaves. If the vines trail along the ground, any part of the plant can be infected if there has been standing water or the leaves have been watered too often. Using a self-watering container is a good way to ensure the plant has plenty of water without watering the foliage. Fertilize with a small amount of slow-release 10-10-10 fertilizer every six weeks.

Cantaloupe plants can be started inside as seedlings and transferred outdoors in the early summer. The plants transplant well when the plant is young, but once it is growing melons, it can be complicated. When moving a seedling from a seed pot into a larger growing pot, give the plant a 5-gallon pot and plan to allow it to grow to its mature size in that pot without another replanting.

Watermelon

Botanical name: *C. lanatus*
Common name: Watermelon
Family name: *Cucurbitaceae*
Origin: Africa
Light: Full sunlight

Size and growth: 10-16' trailing vines

Minimum temperature: 70° Fahrenheit

Blooming season: Summer

Outside hardiness zone: 3-9

Best time to prune: As needed for size

Pests or diseases to watch for: Powdery mildew, aphids, squash bugs, beetles

Fertilizer: 5-10-10

Unique characteristics/growing tips: Dwarf watermelons can be easier to grow in containers. Commercially available watermelon seedlings can grow melons up to 20 pounds. Specialty varieties can grow melons that weigh 100 pounds or more.

Description:

Watermelon plants generally grow to extreme sizes, with 10 to 16 feet being an average vine size. This can make indoor growing difficult. Combined with the large melon size, the difficulty of growing watermelons indoors makes it easier to either place watermelon containers outside or to grow a variety of dwarf watermelon. Like cantaloupes, watermelon plants can be grown in outdoor containers with the vines trailing onto the ground.

Miniature watermelons look and taste like full-sized watermelons, but they are about the size of a softball. The vines grow to approximately 4 to 5 feet in length, fine for indoors or out. Whether it is full size or dwarf, the soil should be enriched with compost when possible, and a 5-10-10 fertilizer should be applied every six weeks. The top of the soil should be mulched with approximately 2 inches of grass clipping, straw, or tree bark. Avoid using pine straw or pine bark with watermelons, as they may add too much acid to the soil.

Watermelons are easy to grow from seeds. They can even be started by placing a seed inside a wet paper towel and placing it in a sunny windowsill. They can be started in seed pots with a small amount of peat moss or potting soil. When transplanting watermelon seedlings, the plant will suffer less transplant shock if the plant is transplanted into a container full of warm, moist soil. Before transplanting, place the larger container in the sun for at least an hour to warm the soil. Moisten the soil slightly before placing the seedling into the new soil.

Watermelon plants are susceptible to aphids and many types of beetles. Beetles can be picked off the plants outdoors, though will likely not be a problem if the plant is grown indoors. Check the plant's leaves for aphids periodically, looking at the stems and under leaves for small dots. Infested leaves can be cut away and removed. Stems that are infested might benefit from being washed with insecticidal soap to kill the insects.

Honeydew

Botanical name: *Cucumis melo*
Common name: Honeydew
Family name: *Cucurbitaceae*
Origin: Europe
Light: Full sunlight
Size and growth: 10'
Minimum temperature: 65° Fahrenheit
Blooming season: Summer
Outside hardiness zone: 3-10
Best time to prune: As needed for size
Pests or diseases to watch for: Powdery mildew, downy mildew, aphids, squash bugs, beetles, snails
Fertilizer: 10-10-10
Unique characteristics/growing tips: Honeydew plants need hot weather, plenty of water, and bees to pollinate the flowers. The seeds can be kept for four years.

Description:

Like other melons, growing honeydew melons indoors can be difficult because of space and weight constraints. They are also picky about their soil conditions; they prefer a soil pH of 6.0 to 7.0.

Dwarf honeydew plants are far easier to grow in containers than the full-size versions. Dwarf plants have 4-foot vines and grow a miniaturized version of the melon that is about 4 inches in diameter. These look and taste the same as full-sized honeydew melons. They need large containers for the vines to sprawl, or they can be trained to climb a trellis. With the small size and weight of the dwarf honeydew, they will not need a fruit hammock to keep them from pulling away from a climbing vine.

Add compost or peat moss to the potting soil mix. Fertilize the plant with 10-10-10 fertilizer every three weeks. If your container is outside, watch the plant closely for pests. Beetles, snails, and caterpillars love honeydew melons, and they will attack them if given the opportunity. Pull off any large bugs and check the leaves for tiny bugs. The rinds of honeydews are relatively soft and are prone to rotting if they are grown on the ground. If your plant trails onto the ground, place something solid, such as plastic or a piece of plywood, under the melons once they appear. This will prevent the rotting common to these melons.

When watering, keep the water off the leaves in order to avoid downy or powdery mildew. Remove any leaves that have a white or gray downy or powdery substance on them. Honeydew plants grown outside and that trail into the grass might have more trouble with fungal diseases and pests. While the melons are growing on the ground, pick them up occasionally as they grow to check for pests on the underside.

Peaches

Botanical name: *P. persica*

Common name: Peach

Family name: *Rosaceae*

Origin: China

Light: Full sunlight

Size and growth: 7-25'

Minimum temperature: -20° Fahrenheit

Blooming season: Spring

Outside hardiness zone: 5-9

Best time to prune: Winter, early spring

Pests or diseases to watch for: Birds

Fertilizer: 10-10-10

Unique characteristics/growing tips: Peach trees need near-freezing temperatures each winter in order to produce fruit. Indoor peach trees should be taken outdoors in the winter.

Description:

A full-size 20- to 25-foot tree would be unmanageable in a planter, but many varieties are dwarf and semi-dwarf sizes. These specialty peach trees might be as small as 5 feet in height. Others grow to 7 to 10 feet and produce a similar peach. The scarlet prince variety grows to 10 to 15 feet in height and 5 to 10 feet in width, is drought tolerant, and is not picky about its soil.

If you purchase a bare-root plant, soak the tree's roots in water for approximately six hours before planting it. Once you plant it in the container, soak the pot with water to help the roots settle in.

Peach trees grown in containers should have a pot approximately 3 feet in diameter to give the roots enough growing room. Peach trees grow rapidly and will produce peaches when they are a few years old. A young seedling might take another three years to produce fruit. If you want peaches right away, choose a tree at least four years old.

A wooden outdoor container, such as a large planter, a barrel, or a crate will have adequate drainage for a peach tree. An indoor container needs gravel in the bottom to enable the soil to drain better. Adding compost to the potting soil will help to nourish the tree. Fertilize the tree every six weeks through the spring and summer with a 10-10-10 fertilizer. Specialized fruit tree fertilizers will also be beneficial. The tree can be pruned in the fall, winter, and early spring before any new growth appears to create the shape and size you want. If the tree is very young, tie it to a stake to help it remain erect.

Peach trees are susceptible to a variety of diseases and pests and should be checked often for fungi and other diseases. Discoloration of the leaves, webs around the leaves, and holes on the leaves are all indications of pests and diseases.

Birds enjoy peaches as much as gardeners do, and a net around the tree can prevent them from pecking at the fruit. Dormant oil spray is an environmentally friendly way to kill and prevent pests and diseases that works well with fruit trees. It is made from oil and soap rather than pesticides or herbicides. It can be made at home or bought from gardening or home improvement stores.

Water the tree regularly; water your tree more often if the container is outside. The soil should not dry out completely in between waterings. Cut away dead branches, and consider cutting away any small, weak branches on an established plant. This will allow the larger branches to grow stronger and produce more fruit.

Strawberries

Botanical name: *F.* × *ananassa*

Common name: Strawberry

Family name: *Rosaceae*

Origin: Europe and North America

Light: Full sunlight

Size and growth: 4-10"

Minimum temperature: 20° Fahrenheit

Blooming season: Spring and summer

Outside hardiness zone: 3-8

Best time to prune: As needed

Pests or diseases to watch for: Snails, slugs, moths, powdery mildew, gray mold, leaf spot

Fertilizer: 10-10-10

Unique characteristics/growing tips: Strawberry plants come in three main varieties, each with its own timetable for fruit production. Choose your type with an eye toward how much space you have and when you want your berries.

Description:

Strawberry plants are easy to grow, they take up little space, and each plant produces a lot of strawberries, so they are an ideal fruit for growing in containers. They can be grown inside or out, and they will grow in a wide variety of planters. Many commercially available varieties are bred to be disease resistant and provide high numbers of berries. The three main types of strawberries are day neutral, everbearing, and June bearing. Each type has its own production time and span and produces a slightly different size, shape, and taste in its strawberries.

Day-neutral strawberry plants are compact plants that produce a small number of runners and produce strawberries from late spring through the summer. These are often chosen for indoor strawberry gardens because of their size and production capabilities. Day-neutral plants are not as particular about the amount of sunlight they receive each day. Other strawberry types need long, sunny days in order to flower and might need a UV lamp indoors if you live in a less-sunny climate. With day neutrals, a sunny windowsill is fine, and a cloudy spring will not stop them from producing.

Everbearing strawberry plants produce several strawberry harvests throughout the year, including one in the fall. They have few runners, which makes them another good indoor fruit plant. Everbearing plants are generally highly disease resistant and grow to about 12 inches in height.

June bearing strawberries produce one larger crop — though it is not in June as the name suggests. These strawberries produce a long spring crop of large berries and propagate themselves with numerous runners. They are good for outdoor containers, but they might take up too much space in an indoor garden after a few years.

Strawberry plants are not particularly fussy about their soil, but they do appreciate good drainage and some sand in the soil. Adding a few handfuls of sand will accomplish both of these goals. Planting at least three to four strawberry plants will allow for pollination between them. Add compost, peat moss, or manure to the soil to add to the nutrients in the soil.

Specialized strawberry containers with side spouts built in for strawberry runners are available. These make it easy to have a large crop of berries from one small pot. Outdoors, a long, rectangular container is often chosen to allow strawberry plants to spread their runners.

In their first year, the flowers on June-bearing plants should be removed to allow for more growth, a better future crop, and a longer production life. For everbearing and day-neutral plants, remove all of the flowers through June, allowing the flowers to remain from July on. This will accomplish the same expanded growth for those varieties.

Mulch the top of the soil with a non-pine mulch to keep the soil and roots cool. This will also keep moisture in the soil and the berries from having too much contact with the soil. Because you are using potting soil, contact will not result in many pests or bacteria, but the moisture can lead to the fruit going bad sooner than it should.

Water the soil every day to keep it lightly moist. Many varieties of strawberry plants are susceptible to powdery mildew and other fungi. To minimize the danger of these diseases, water the soil instead of the foliage. Watch for any discolorations of the leaves, stems, and berries. Each is susceptible to molds and rotting diseases on non-resistant plants. Add some 10-10-10 fertilizer into the soil when planting and again in the early summer. Fertilizing too often, however, can lead to too many leaves and too few flowers. If you live in a cold climate, do not fertilize your plants in the fall or the plants might start new growth at a time when it will be most susceptible to damage.

June-bearing strawberry plants might need pruning to keep their size in check. Newer runners can be cut away if you want to keep the plant within its container. Runners that have put down roots can be cut out and transplanted into a new container. Cut away any dead leaves, and remove any plants that have stopped producing strawberries. Some varieties will only produce for three or four years, so watch for production. If the season has come and one plant is not producing, consider cutting a rooted runner from another plant and using that to replace the non-bearing plant.

Watch outdoor strawberry plants closely for pests, particularly after a heavy rain. Snails and slugs will quickly chew holes in strawberries, and they might hide on the underside to avoid detection. If your containers are close to the ground, do a quick inspection every once in a while to ensure the container has not become infested. One small slug can render several berries inedible.

Tomatoes

Botanical name: *Solanum lycopersicum*

Common name: Tomato

Family name: *Solanaceae*

Origin: South America

Light: Full sun

Size and growth: 1-8' in height

Minimum temperature: 40° Fahrenheit

Blooming season: Summer

Outside hardiness zone: 3-11

Best time to prune: Prune weak stems when they appear. Determinate varieties should be pruned of dead foliage only.

Pests or diseases to watch for: Cutworms, slugs, fungi

Fertilizer: 10-10-10 fertilizer

Unique characteristics/growing tips: Most varieties need support to keep the plants upright.

Description:

Most home gardeners start by growing tomatoes. Tomatoes are popular among home-growers for a number of reasons including the ease of growth, abundance of tomatoes grown by each plant, and compact size of many tomato plant varieties. Very

Young tomato plants are grown indoors.
Picture by Lizz Shepherd

little room is needed to grow many tomatoes. Miniature tomato plants can be as small as one foot in height, producing many small, round tomatoes.

Tomatoes come in yellow, orange, white, red, pink, green, and purple varieties. Each type has its own flavor, which ranges from sweet to lemony to bitter. As a home gardener, you can choose from hundreds of types of tomatoes. If you prefer large tomato slices, you might choose to grow a beefsteak tomato. Beefsteak tomatoes can weigh a pound or more, can be sliced thick enough to grill, and are favored by many tomato lovers. If you primarily want small salad tomatoes, try a variety of cherry or grape tomatoes. If you dislike the taste of commercial tomatoes, try lollipop cherry tomatoes for their lemon flavor.

Tomatoes grow well from both seed and transplanted young plants. The size of the container needed depends on the tomato variety. Seeds can be started in a seed flat and transplanted to a larger pot as needed. Because they grow so quickly, tomatoes can outgrow their pots and need larger ones before they are mature. Watch for bound roots as tomato plants mature.

If you will keep your tomato containers outdoors, make sure the last freeze of the year has passed. If you have any variety of tomato plant larger than a cherry or grape tomato plant, you will need to support the stems of the plant. Tomato cages are round, wire supports that can be put around the container to hold up the stems when they form. A trellis may also work if the stems are tied to it as they grow; however, stakes are better than trellises for tomato plants.

Tomato plants need full sunlight and should be watered often. They will likely need water every day, particularly if they are outside or already bearing tomatoes. If the plants are outdoors, elevating the pot might discourage slugs from finding the plants. You can also bring containers inside to avoid an unseasonably cold night; frost can quickly kill a tomato plant.

Use a balanced fertilizer, such as 10-10-10, when you transplant the tomato plants and every few weeks after that. Any time you add fertilizer, avoid touching the stems or leaves with the fertilizer. This can burn the plant and cause serious damage. To prevent fungal growth, water the soil instead of the leaves and stems. If you see a leaf with white or black discoloration, cut off the leaf and dispose of it to avoid spreading the fungal infection.

If a tomato plant suffers from frequent fungal infections, the plant might not have adequate air circulation. Try moving the pot and allowing more space around it. If that does not cure the problem, the plant might have been watered too often. When a tomato is ripe, it can be pulled away from the stem by hand or the stem can be cut with a pair of pruners.

Common Mistakes to Avoid when Growing Fruit

Because fruit plants need so much sunlight, one common mistake is not allowing enough of it to come into direct contact with the plant each day. Other than currants and day neutral strawberry plants, all of the fruit plants discussed here need many hours of sunlight each day in order to produce their fruit. In some climates, getting a UV lamp can help an entire room of fruit-bearing plants get the sunlight they need. An outdoor porch or patio might be best for many fruit plants because of their heat and sunlight requirements.

Growing citrus trees can be complicated by their general need for moisture and humidity. Some require a great deal of maintenance, such as regular pruning, misting, and inspecting for disease and mites. They can also grow to large sizes, which makes it difficult to move them indoors when needed. Before choosing a fruit tree for a container, consider whether you have the space and time needed to keep them healthy and productive.

Fruit plants that do not need high humidity or misting often suffer from both a high need for water and a susceptibility to mildew and fungi from having too much moisture. This can be a delicate balance to achieve, and it requires careful watering procedures to ensure the water stays in the soil and not on the green parts of the plant. If you live in a hot climate and keep your fruit plants outdoors, water them in the early morning or late evening to prevent the water converting to a hot steam that can injure the plants. This also ensures the water stays in the soil for a longer period of time.

Although some fruit plants, such as citrus trees, need a high-acid soil, many do not. A fruit plant such as a strawberry plant can be killed by a soil that is too acidic. To avoid too much acid, avoid pine needle mulch in plants that do not need a high acid level. If you are in doubt about the pH level of your soil or how acidic you have made your soil, use a soil pH kit to be sure. It is better to spend a little extra time and money to ensure the right soil conditions than to lose your plants altogether.

When reusing your plant containers for new plants, be sure to wash your containers thoroughly with detergent and rinse away all of the detergent. Most fruit plants are so susceptible to mildew and other plant diseases easily passed on from an old pot to a new plant.

Consider how much space a mature plant takes up. Even a smaller plant, such as a June bearing strawberry plant, can take up an enormous amount of space after a few years. If you are growing inside an apartment or small house, fruit plants like grape plants might simply take up too much space for your indoor environment.

Some varieties need to be pollinated by other plants, bees, or butterflies within the same plant. If you do not have the time to pollinate a plant, choose a self-pollinating plant or plant several plants together. Fruit trees are particularly in need of other trees to pollinate them if they are not self-pollinating. Without the proper pollination, fruit cannot be produced.

It might sound too complicated, but often this can be taken care of by growing several containers of a small species, such as strawberries together, or taking trees outdoors in the spring to allow nature to take care of the process. A tiny fruit tree like a dwarf lemon or lime tree can be pollinated in a few sessions with a paintbrush.

Fruits such as full-size melons often need special arrangements when grown indoors or on an outdoor trellis. Trellising is a good space saver, but it can lead to problems when the fruit grow in and each need to be individually supported. As each fruit grows, it must be support by something breathable and flexible to allow it to grow while having its weight supported by the material. Old pantyhose, mesh bags and other materials can be used to make a supportive hammock by tying them around the fruit and attaching them to the trellis.

Be sure to match the fertilizer and the need for organic materials with the type of fruit plant you grow. The fertilizer each requires is based on its precise needs from the soil. Although some fruit plants do fine without having any extra organic materials added to the soil, others might suffer without those added nutrients.

CASE STUDY:
GARDENING THROUGH
THE YEARS

Hanna Rhoades
ThisGardenIsIllegal.com, blogger
hannamyluv@gmail.com
www.thisgardenisillegal.com
Phone: (440) 227-3620

I started gardening for myself in containers when I was in college and have kept a container garden ever since. I have been gardening in containers for 15 years.

The original advantage I found with container gardens was the fact that they are portable. College students have a housing record much akin to gypsies, and it was not uncommon for me to move every few months or so when I was in college. My little container garden could be packed up and moved with me.

When I finally settled down a bit, I was living in an apartment and containers were perfect for allowing me to have a small garden despite my meagerness in the workable land department.

Later, after I bought my house, I began to love the fact I could grow exotic plants, such as oranges, brugmansias, and bay trees. I haul — OK, my husband hauls — them in and out every year, but it is worth it when you see people gape at the fact you have a tree full of oranges on your front porch.

Judging from my own experience, I think people choose to grow food indoors because they do not have much choice. Most people lack either space or the environment to grow what they want, and they either grow plants indoors or do not grow plants at all. For a diehard gardener, not growing plants is simply not an option.

The main problems with indoor container gardening are light and space. You only have so many windows in the house, and you can only have so many plants placed in the windows. You can supplement with fluorescent lighting, but even then, there are only so many shop lights your spouse will allow you to hang around the house.

In the winter, when my entire container garden is indoors, it looks like a refugee camp for plants. They are huddled around windows or cramped under the makeshift light of cheap shop lights hung from the ceiling.

People are more interested now in growing their own food due to several factors. First, people realized their kids have no idea where their food comes from. Their children think it magically turns into pizzas and pastries, and with today's food chemistry, they are probably not far off the mark. Growing even a little bit of food, such as a pot of mint or a tomato plant, allows kids to see food starts as something real. It starts a conversation on it. I always kind of thought this was the botanical version of getting your kids a girl and boy hamster in order to help you have "The Talk."

Second, cooking is making a big comeback thanks to the media. Rock star chefs are espousing about fresh and local and unusual or heirloom varieties just not available at your nearest grocery store. For many people, the only way they can have access to these ingredients is to grow the foods themselves.

Third, the economy is driving people back to gardening in droves. When before, $3 to $4 for tiny handful of basil was no big deal, now that $3 to $4 can mean the difference between the car getting gas or not. A $2 packet of basil that will help you grow basil year round, or at least during the summer, looks like a real bargain. We are remembering what good food tastes like, and we will not let a silly thing like a recession get in the way of that luxury — especially considering we have figured out the "luxury" of good food does not need to cost a lot of money.

Fourth, baby boomers are just reaching "that age." Gardening in earnest is something that requires time. When you are younger and you have family, work and financial constraints weighing on you, it is hard to dedicate much time to playing in the dirt. Baby boomers, a giant bulge in the generational population, are watching as their children fly from the nest, their companies throw them retirement parties, and their social security, pensions, and 401(k)s reach eligibility. They look around and think "What now?" Then, they see the sun and the flowers and remember what a real tomato tastes like. They know what to do next. Interest in gardening as a hobby happens to every generation at this age, but the baby boomer generation is so big it is bringing a completely new focus to the game.

The main advantage of growing your own food is control — plain and simple. Control over what is grown, how it is grown, and what it is exposed to while it is grown.

Spider mites are the bane of my indoor gardening existence. Although it is technically a pesticide — but an organic, safe, man-made, and chemical-free pesticide — I found neem oil last winter and now use it on everything. It has been used in India for years for *everything* from medicine to cosmetics to pesticide and is now getting popular in the United States.

The other thing you can do to keep plants from needing pesticide in the first place is to keep you plants healthy. Pests attack plants more often when the plants are stressed. Proper care will help keep pests away.

Chapter 10

GROWING FLOWERS IN CONTAINERS

Many home gardeners get their start with container flowers because so many common varieties grow well with little care and take up a small amount of space. Even kids can grow flowers in containers if given the proper tools. With a container, some potting soil and fertilizer, and a window to the outside, a small space can come alive with color and fragrance.

Although there are many hardy flowers that can grow indoors or out with little care and with few special supplies, there are also many that require special tools and a variety of interventions to keep them healthy. Orchids, for example, need specialized care, staking, and frequent fertilization to produce flowers. Gloxinias need a high humidity level to keep them healthy and are often placed on a tray of water to keep the humidity around them high enough.

Can You Grow Any Type of Flowers in Containers?

Virtually any flower can be grown in a container. Some are larger than others, such as a large flowering bush, and might require an outdoor container. However, most of the plants people are familiar with do not need a container much larger than a large indoor plant pot. There are flowers that can be grown in a 4-inch pot, flowers that require a container the size of a 5-gallon bucket, and everything in between.

Large containers can be used to grow several types of flowers or different colors of the same flower type. Some people put together their own flower gardens in large outdoor planters or smaller ones that house several plants. These arrangements can also be bought from nurseries and home improvement stores. Some people find arranging and designing indoor gardens to be a fun and relaxing way to indulge their creativity and decorate their homes for little money.

Why Grow Your Own Flowers?

Flowers are generally easy to grow and easy to preserve. They can be grown by hobbyists of any skill level. You do not need to know a lot about flowers or have previous experience with houseplants in order to grow beautiful flowering plants.

There are many ways to use flowers in your home décor. Even if your budget is tiny, you can have elegant décor with the right plants. Flowers never go out of style. Attractive flowers do not have to be changed with the next home decorating trend like many decorative items do. They can serve as a hint of color in a neutral room, a way to add to a color scheme, or a focal point for any room for years to come with very little expense.

Flowers can give your front yard curb appeal and your backyard a more attractive feel. They can dress up your porch or patio and provide something to look forward to in the spring and summer. They can also be cut and used in a vase to beautify your dinner table and can be given as gifts.

If you are interested in growing food at home, you might decide to start with flowers to get a feel for what plants need to grow in containers and gain confidence in your ability to care for them. They also provide a way to cleanse the indoor air and clear out indoor air pollution. Fragrant varieties provide a fresh scent to your home without paying for chemical fragrances that can be expensive and toxic to the air. Some people even grow flowers at home as a small home business, selling cut flower arrangements at local farmers markets, at roadside stands, and to neighborhood customers.

A Complete List of Container-grown Flowers

The following flower types are common and can be found in local nurseries or grown from seed. All are small enough to be grown in containers and few need a lot of special attention to keep them growing and producing flowers.

Roses

Botanical name: *Rosa*

Common name: Rose

Family name: *Rosaceae*

Origin: Asia, Africa, Europe, North America

Light: Full sunlight

Size and growth: 10"-5'

Minimum temperature: -10° Fahrenheit

Blooming season: Spring and summer

Outside hardiness zone: 3-11

Best time to prune: Spring

Pests or diseases to watch for: Aphids, leafhoppers, spider mites, slugs, snails, powdery mildew, blackspot fungus

Fertilizer: 7-8-5

Unique characteristics/growing tips: With hundreds of varieties available, choose from a wide variety of rose sizes and colors. Roses need constant moisture and sunny but cool conditions.

Description:

Roses are a popular container plant for their intricate flowers and lovely smell. Many roses sold by florists have little or no fragrance and instead are grown for their hardiness and ability to stay fresh long after being cut. These are not usually grown for their fragrance or interesting petal shapes and colors. As a home grower, choose from hundreds of different types of roses for their smell, color, size, or shape. Decide between thorny and thornless varieties and white, ivory, yellow, peach, orange, pink, red, or purple. Some have little fragrance, some have a noticeable fragrance when you get close to them, and some will scent several rooms with their sweet scent. There are miniature rose varieties that reach one foot or less in height, and there are rose bushes that grow to approximately 5 feet in height.

There are three main types of roses: modern garden, old garden, and wild roses. Modern garden roses are newer varieties developed in 1867 and later. These roses are sought after for their striking colors and large blooms, and they have long been the most popular type of roses for home gardeners. These come in many different types, including hybrid tea roses and floribunda. Hybrid tea roses are usually the ones grown by florists.

Wild roses, also known as species roses, are the oldest varieties, often found growing wild in rainy areas and as meadow flowers. They are types that have never been cultivated by humans for different characteristics, and they look a little different from the flowers most people are used to calling roses. Wild roses have only five petals and a larger open area in the center. Most wild roses are pink, with a few varieties of white, yellow, and red growing worldwide.

Old garden roses are cultivated rose types that have been around since before 1867. Tea roses, bourbons, chinas, and noisettes are all types of old garden roses These often have a different shape from florist roses, with a "shaggier" shape composed of more petals. Some varieties of old garden rose have 100 petals or more.

All of these rose types can be grown in containers with a high-quality potting soil, regular fertilization, and enough water to keep a steady level of moisture. The container you choose for a full-sized rose plant should be at least 15 to 20 inches in diameter. Rose plants have intricate roots and need plenty of room to stretch them. If they should get root bound, they will suffer from nutrient and moisture stress. The container should begin with potting soil and a few extra elements to make it suitable for roses. Add some 7-8-5 fertilizer and compost together in the beginning. Bone meal, fish meal, and blood meal are also fertilizers often used for roses.

Approximately one cup of perlite can also be added to the soil in order to help maintain the constant moisture roses need. Although it sounds like a contradiction, too much moisture on the plant's roots can cause serious problems in roses, such as root rot. To prevent too much water on the roots, place some gravel at the bottom of the pot to allow for more drainage.

Although roses need full sunlight, they do not like high temperatures. If you are going to keep your rose plant outside during hot, sunny weather, place it in a light-colored container. A darker one can capture the heat from the sun and cause the soil's temperature to climb too high. Expect to re-pot your rose plant every two to three years unless you choose a miniature variety.

Roses need to be watered often, so check the soil several times per week to see whether it needs moisture. Roses also need a lot of air circulation to keep them from falling victim to fungi. Place the container away from walls, fences, other plants, and anything that will keep air from moving around them. Their placement should also afford them six to seven hours of sunlight per day. In the spring, mix in a little bit of Epsom salt into the soil to give the plant the magnesium roses need during the beginning of their growing season to grow new foliage.

Pruning of roses should only take place before the newest spring growth appears. If you prune your bushes in the fall, it can stimulate new growth, and the new growth will then be susceptible to the cold of the winter, killing off parts of the stems. Pruning should also be done whenever there are dead leaves, dead flowers, or areas infested with mildew. Because roses are inedible, you might choose to use pesticides on them to keep aphids and other pests at bay.

Small rose varieties can be kept in hanging baskets, kept in small indoor or outdoor containers, or planted together in groups in large planters. Miniature roses can be as small as 10 inches in height, and they can be kept in tiny spaces anywhere with a sunny window. They need similar soil and light conditions as larger roses. Miniature roses are perfect for hanging baskets and found-object containers, such as boots, old tubes, or any other object a plant can be placed into.

Gardeners who have good luck with their roses sometimes turn them into a larger hobby, attending rose shows, entering rose-growing contests, and joining local rose-enthusiast clubs. If you are good at growing roses, you can even develop your own color hybrid by breeding different rose colors together, which you then get to choose a name for.

Flowers from bulbs

Planting flower bulbs is an easy way to start new flowers from scratch. Unlike seeds, bulbs do not need much care and maintenance to get them to grow. Flowers that grow from bulbs are often exotic-looking flowers that grow easily and in little time. Some larger varieties, such as gladiolus, however, do need to be staked to keep them standing upright.

When you plant flower bulbs, you have to orient the bulb properly to get it to grow upward through the soil. Every flower bulb has a pointy end. For some bulbs, this might be hard to discern at first, and in others one end of the bulb will form a sharp point. The leaves grow out of that point, so it must be arranged in the soil with that point upward.

Although each flower bulb has its own specific soil depth at which it needs to be planted, the general rule is to plant it 2 ½ times as deep as the height

Hyacinth flowers and bulbs

of the bulb. If the bulb is 2 inches tall, plant it 5 inches deep unless you have bulbs that come with instructions that say otherwise.

Another rule of thumb is to mix a little bit of bulb food into the potting soil when you plant a bulb. Be sure to mix it well, or the fertilizer could burn the bulb.

Water the soil well, and place mulch over the soil to keep it moist. Place the container in a sunny location and wait for it to grow. Water it whenever the soil feels dry. Depending on the type of flower you are growing and the time of year it is, it might be a few days to a few weeks before you see growth break the surface of the mulch.

Bulbs generally grow long, slender stalks that have one flower or a larger, compound flower. This often inspires an elegant presentation for the resulting flowers, such as one single bulb planted in a glazed, 12-inch pot. A single flower in a small pot allows you to place multiple bulb pots around your home or outdoor space. Another representation is to use a larger container such as a long rectangular plant and to plant your bulbs in a row. A window flower box is the perfect place to plant a row of bulbs.

Daffodils

Botanical name: *Narcissus*

Common name: Daffodil

Family name: *Amaryllidaceae*

Origin: Southern Europe, Asia

Light: Full sunlight

Size and growth: 2"-2'

Minimum temperature: -40° Fahrenheit

Blooming season: Spring and summer

Outside hardiness zone: 3-10

Best time to prune: Summer

Pests or diseases to watch for: None

Fertilizer: 5-10-10

Unique characteristics/growing tips: Fertilize in the spring. Bulbs need to be divided every few years.

Description:

Daffodils are easy to grow and perfect for a new bulb planter. They are most famous for their bright yellow variety, but there are many more colors from which to choose. Orange, white, peach, and many other daffodil colors are available. Daffodil bulbs divide themselves, and a large pot can eventually grow many daffodils all from a single bulb. Daffodils can also be grown from seed, but the seeds can take as long as five years to grow.

There are also several daffodil sizes from which to choose. Miniature versions have flowers as small as half an inch across that grow on 2-inch stems. The larger varieties grow to 2 feet high and bloom with 5-inch flowers. When grown in the ground, they generally have to be planted in the fall with blooming expected in the spring. However, by growing them in containers, they can be grown indoors at any time of year, or they can be started indoors and taken outside once the weather is warm. Daffodil bulbs, even under the ground, need sunlight in order to bloom.

After a daffodil has bloomed and the flower has died, cut the dead flower away, but leave the foliage in place if you want flowers again the next year. During that time, the plant will start preparing for the next year's growth and will be storing nutrients from its foliage.

Daffodils need good drainage and slightly acidic soil. They should be watered lightly every day, and more heavily if they are kept outdoors. Fertilize with organic matter when planting. Daffodils will reproduce in the form of multiple bulbs called "daughter" bulbs underground. Every few years, dig up the bulbs and divide them or they may become too numerous for your pot. Daffodils are largely resistant to pests.

Tulips

Botanical name: *Tulipa*
Common name: Tulip
Family name: *Liliaceae*
Origin: Europe, Asia, Africa
Light: Full sunlight
Size and growth: 12-16"
Minimum temperature: -25° Fahrenheit
Blooming season: Spring
Outside hardiness zone: 3-8
Best time to prune: Summer
Pests or diseases to watch for: Aphids, deer
Fertilizer: 9-9-6
Unique characteristics/growing tips: Deadhead the flowers when they die, and remove yellowed foliage as it fades in the late spring.

Description:

Tulips can be planted in the same container with other bulb flowers, or they can be planted alone in small containers. Tulips come in a wide range of colors and shapes, and they are often grown in containers because of their compact size. To start growing tulips, add some compost or other organic material to the pot and mix it well. They do not like compacted, heavy soil, so keep it loose for aeration. Coffee grounds can be used in place of compost because they deliver nitrogen to the soil. The top of the soil should be lightly mulched to hold moisture. Tulips like a slightly acidic soil, so adding a few pine needles into the mulch can help to take the pH level to 6.0 to 6.5, which is what tulips prefer.

Most tulip bulbs are large and are planted deeply, so water the bulbs well to make sure the moisture reaches the bulb. Before the bulbs break the surface, water them approximately twice a week. Be sure the pot has good drainage or the bulb could rot or develop a fungal infection. Adding a little bit of sand to the soil will help with drainage.

If you are planting a row of bulbs in a planter, plant them at least 5 inches apart to allow them each enough sunlight and air circulation. They need full sunlight and hot conditions to grow well. If you live in a hot, sunny climate, they will tolerate shade for part of the day. Before planting your bulbs, keep them at a cool, non-freezing temperature until they are planted. Keeping them in the refrigerator is best. If you want to grow them outdoors, plant them in the fall in outdoor planters, and they will bloom in the spring.

When the shoots surface, water them every few days, but keep the moisture away from the foliage. Then, when the flower eventually dies and turns yellow, cut away the flower. If the dead flower is allowed to remain on the stalk, it will produce seeds. If you keep the plant from putting down seeds and you allow the stems and leaves to die on its own, you can expect the bulb to grow again the following year. Once all of the foliage is dead and turns a thorough yellow, cut it away and allow the bulb to stay in the container for the following year if you want the flower to sprout again. If you want to reuse the pot for something that will give you foliage and/or flowers in the winter, dig up the bulb and keep it in the refrigerator over the winter. Many gardeners discard their older bulbs in the fall, treating the plants as annuals and replacing them with new tulip varieties in the spring.

Fertilize tulips in the spring to promote growth, and if they are to be left in a container throughout the winter, fertilize them again in the fall to keep them healthy during their dormancy in the cold season. During that dormant period, do not water them. Watering them will make them unreliable sprouters and may lead to the rotting of the bulb.

Aphids can be a problem for tulips, but they can be washed away with insecticidal soap or a strong stream of water. Tulips are a favorite flower of deer, and precautions, such as fencing, can be taken in areas where deer are a problem.

Amaryllis

Botanical name: *Amaryllis belladonna*
Common name: Amaryllis
Family name: *Amarylidaceae*
Origin: South America, Africa
Light: Full sunlight to partial sunlight
Size and growth: 1-2'
Minimum temperature: 60° Fahrenheit
Blooming season: Winter
Outside hardiness zone: 9-11
Best time to prune: Spring
Pests or diseases to watch for: Aphids, spider mites, caterpillars
Fertilizer: 10-60-10
Unique characteristics/growing tips: Amaryllis plants have an unusual shape; they bloom on a long stalk free of leaves.

Description:

Amaryllis plants are known for their large, colorful blooms and lack of leaves and stems once the flowers bloom. One single trunk grows to a height of 18 to 24 inches tall. Several large flowers grow on the single trunk, and there are many bright colors from which to choose. The best-known colors are bright red and deep orange, but there are also white, purple, and pink varieties available. The tall stalk and simple foliage make this an elegant-looking plant that is compact enough to fit onto even the smallest table.

Amaryllis bulbs are often given as Christmas presents because they bloom well indoors and can be grown throughout the year. The flowers last for

approximately seven weeks, and can be as large as 6 inches across. Amaryllis kits are sold that come with a container already filled with potting soil and a planted bulb. With these kits, you simply need to water the soil as directed and watch the flower grow.

If you are not starting with a prefilled amaryllis kit, start with a pot at least 5 inches in diameter. Unlike most large flower bulbs, the bulb is not planted at a depth 2 ½ times the size of the bulb. It is planted just below the surface of the soil, with the pointy end of the bulb just above the surface. Water the bulb well the first time, and soak the soil. Keep the container in a sunny place and water the soil whenever it feels dry. Fertilize lightly with a water-soluble fertilizer once a month.

The plant will grow a few flat leaves as the central stalk grows, but it will generally lose those before the flowers bloom. The stalk may need to be staked to keep it upright. Some larger plants might slump over if they are not staked. Another issue is a leaning stalk trying to capitalize on the sunlight exposure it has. Turning the pot twice a week will give it uniform sun exposure and keep the stalk straight.

Once the flowers have died, the plant should be pruned. Cut away the stalk all the way to the top of the bulb. If you want it to grow again the next year, keep the bulb in the pot and water it occasionally to keep it from drying out. Avoid keeping the bulb moist, however, or it could rot.

If you want your amaryllis to bloom at a specific time, such as the holidays, you can force the bulb to bloom. To force a blooming, cut away the flowers after the blooming has stopped, but allow the stalk to remain. Place the container in a sunny area and continue to water the soil. Stop watering the plant about 12 weeks before you want it to bloom again, and place it in a cool area about 60 degrees Fahrenheit. The foliage will die, and the plant will start sprouting a new stalk. Once the new stalk begins to grow, water the plant again and place it in a sunny location. The stalk will continue to grow and produce new flowers about 12 weeks after the process began.

If you have an amaryllis that never blooms, it might not have enough sunlight to produce flowers. It also might not have a rich-enough soil. Add some gentle, water-soluble fertilizer every three weeks to attempt to stimulate growth, and give it more hours of sun each day. Check it periodically for aphids, and use a wet cloth, insecticidal soap, or a spray of water to remove them.

Hyacinth

Botanical name: *Hyacinthus*
Common name: Hyacinth
Family name: *Hyacinthaceae*
Origin: Mediterranean
Light: Full sunlight to partial sunlight
Size and growth: 12"

Minimum temperature: 20° Fahrenheit

Blooming season: Spring

Outside hardiness zone: 4-9

Best time to prune: Fall

Pests or diseases to watch for: Aphids

Fertilizer: None

Unique characteristics/growing tips: In outdoor containers, plant a few weeks before a freeze.

Description:

Hyacinth plants are short and compact, and they produce a spectacular array of bell-shaped flowers that grow on a central spike. The plant reaches a mature height of about 6 to 12 inches. The flowers are fragrant and come in white, yellow, pink, orange, red, purple, and more. The plants grow seven or eight deep-green leaves that ring the central stalk.

If you want to keep hyacinth containers outside, place the bulbs outdoors in the fall about one to two months before the first hard freeze. This can be anywhere between September and November, depending on your local climate. Plant the bulbs about 6 inches deep, with multiple bulbs planted about 6 inches apart.

Hyacinth jars, also called forcing jars, are a specialized type of container that will grow a hyacinth from a bulb with no soil. The hourglass shape of these containers holds the bulb securely while the plant's roots reach the water at the bottom of the container. These containers are interesting to look at and will grow a hyacinth with minimum fuss.

Water the bulbs after planting them, and from then on, water them regularly. Never allow the soil to become completely dry. After the flowers have bloomed, allow the plant to continue growing until the foliage dies. After the blooms have died, the plant still needs to take in energy from the sun and store it in its bulb. Cutting the foliage down early will interfere with this arrangement. After the foliage has completely died, cut away the plant at its base, leaving the bulb in place. Once a year, apply compost to the potting soil. In later years, the size of the flowers might get smaller, so some hyacinth growers treat these plants as annuals and get a new plant every one to two years.

These flowers make good container plants for window boxes, small spaces, and larger, outdoor planters. They can be planted alongside other bulb flowers, such as tulips, to create a varied flower garden in a large container. The soil should be slightly sandy with a small amount of organic material, such as peat moss.

Like the amaryllis, the hyacinth can be forced to bloom at a specific time by changing the plant's conditions. To make the plant bloom in the winter, keep watering the plant while it is flowering. Keep the soil lightly moist at all times, but do not fertilize it. Then, after the flowers and foliage have died, place the container in the refrigerator. This will speed up the development of the roots so the plant will bloom before it would have otherwise been ready. For many hyacinth bulbs, this requires approximately three months of cold temperatures and no light. You can put the bulb in a bag, in a forcing jar, or keep it in a pot of soil when you are forcing it to bloom.

If you are using a forcing jar, fill the bottom portion of the jar with water, but keep the water from touching the bulb. The plant will develop roots that will reach the water, but keeping the bulb in contact with the water can cause rot. When the water runs low, add more until it is high enough to be close to the bulb without touching it. If you keep your bulbs in the refrigerator, do not keep them near fruit. Fruit gives off a gas that can damage or even kill flower bulbs like hyacinths and amaryllis. Keep the bulbs in a separate container, or keep the fruit in a bag to contain the gas. When the plant gets to be approximately 2 inches tall, take the jar out of the refrigerator and place it in an area that has a little light exposure, but not full sunlight. After a few days, move it to a sunnier spot and enjoy the blooms that appear. For a longer blooming period, give your hyacinth cooler temperatures of 60 to 65 degrees. You can force your hyacinths to bloom again and again, with several bloom periods per year by using this method.

Gladiolus

Botanical name: *Gladiolus*

Common name: Gladiolus, sword lily

Family name: *Iridaceae*

Origin: Asia, Africa, Europe

Light: Full sunlight

Size and growth: 2-5'

Minimum temperature: 10° Fahrenheit

Blooming season: Summer

Outside hardiness zone: 6-10

Best time to prune: Late summer

Pests or diseases to watch for: Dry rot

Fertilizer: 5-10-5

Unique characteristics/growing tips: The tall, thin stalks of gladiolus plants generally need to be staked to keep them from falling over.

Description:

Gladiolus plants were once widely popular, grown in virtually every home garden until first lady Jackie Kennedy announced her dislike for them. Although they fell out of favor for several decades, they are making a comeback as home gardeners see how easy they are to grow, how hardy the plants are, and how many lovely flowers they produce on their tall, elaborate stalks.

If you have the vertical space, gladiolus plants can be grown indoors in a small container. In a pot 10 inches across or larger, use potting soil, at least one cup of organic material, such as peat moss, and a handful of sand that

are well mixed together to start your bulb. The sand is helpful for drainage, but it is not a vital part of the soil. If you have only potting soil and do not have organic materials or sand to add, gladiolus will still grow and bloom.

Plant the bulb 2 ½ times as deep as the size of the bulb, and water the soil well. Gladiolus plants generally do need staking unless you are growing them next to a tall surface the plant can lean on. Some gardeners choose to place a stake at the same time they plant the bulb to avoid injuring the roots the bulb will eventually put down. Or, you can wait and watch the plant and add a stake to the pot only if the plant needs one.

The planted bulb will need full sunlight and good drainage in order to sprout. Like other bulbs, too much water for too long a time will cause the bulb to rot. Avoid using manure on the bulbs, as it can also cause bulb rot. Much the top of the soil to hold in moisture, but do not use pine needles as mulch. Wood chips or straw work well for these plants. Begin planting gladiolus in outdoor containers in the middle of spring, and you will have blooms by early summer. It generally takes about 70 to 100 days for the planted bulbs to sprout, grow, and bloom. The flowers will generally last for a few of weeks as long as the plant is being grown under the right conditions. You can fertilize your gladiolus as soon as the flowers appear in order to increase the plant's vigor.

Water your gladiolus often; keep the soil lightly moist. If you are growing one of the taller gladiolus varieties, the plants will likely need to be tied to a stake to keep them upright. The stalks of gladiolus can be quite thick, so orchid clips are generally not large enough to hold the plants onto the stakes. You might choose colorful string or yarn, or for a less conspicuous tie, use either green thread that matches the foliage or clear string. Do not tie the plant tightly enough to cut into the foliage. Rather, create a loop that will hold the plant up without constricting it. The object is really to keep the plant from falling over not to hold it tightly to the stake.

To keep your gladiolus bulbs for the next year, let them stay in the pot and place them in a cool place until the spring. Or, dig them out of the soil after the plant's foliage has died and store them out of the soil. After the flowers have died, cut away everything except 1 inch of the foliage. This will allow you to reuse your pot while the bulb has gone dormant. To keep the bulb until the spring, dig the bulb out of the soil, and lay it out to dry; it should not be stored wet. Then, keep the bulb in the cold and dark for a few months to make it go dormant. A dark place in the refrigerator or a box in a cool garage will work.

Outdoors, gladiolus can be grown well in zones five through 11, with some varieties having a more restricted zone range, and the outdoor pots can be left outside during the cold weather in order to create the dormancy that will allow the plant to come back again the following spring. In general, gladiolus are one of the easiest and long-lasting bulbs to grow, and they create one of the largest flower arrays of common garden bulbs.

Lily

Botanical name: *Lilium*
Common name: Lily
Family name: *LIliaceae*
Origin: Europe, Asia
Light: Full sunlight
Size and growth: 2-5'
Minimum temperature: 45° Fahrenheit
Blooming season: Spring, summer

Outside hardiness zone: 3-9

Best time to prune: Fall

Pests or diseases to watch for: Lily beetles, aphids, basil rot

Fertilizer: 5-10-10

Unique characteristics/growing tips: Lily bulbs divide underground and should be dug up and separated every other year.

Description:

Lilies are an extremely versatile plant, with an enormous variety of colors, sizes, shapes, and scents available. They are generally tall and colorful, with everything from solid-color to striped to polka dot varieties available. Although they are mostly tall, they grow well in containers and need little horizontal space. The container should be at least 10 inches in diameter. This will allow the bulb to be planted as deeply as it needs to be, as a pot's depth and diameter at the top are the same. These large bulbs need to be planted about 4 to 6 inches deep, depending on the size of the bulb. If you are growing taller lilies and want to keep them outdoors, they might need to be staked to avoid being knocked over by wind gusts.

When planting lily bulbs, add a small amount of slow-release, granulated fertilizer to the potting soil. If your outdoor lilies are in danger of a frost, bring them inside to protect them from the weather. Temperatures below zero will kill lilies.

If you keep your lily bulbs in their pots during the winter, water them only lightly. The bulbs are particularly susceptible to rot during this time. The soil should not be allowed to dry out fully, but avoid soil any more than lightly moist. The dormant bulbs should be kept in a cool, dry place. When the weather gets warmer, allow the bulbs to stay in a warmed place, but one with little sun. When the new shoots are about 3 inches high, they can be given full sun again.

Some lily varieties multiply their bulbs under the soil quickly. These varieties need to be dug up every two or three years so some of the bulbs can be removed. Surprise lilies and Asiatic lilies are both fast multipliers that might need to be re-potted or divided every other year.

Fertilizer made for tomatoes can be used with lilies every few weeks during the blooming season of summer. Lilies can be fertilized as often as every two weeks during the summer, but they will likely not need it that often if slow-release fertilizer was mixed into the soil when you first potted the bulb. If the leaves remain a deep green in color, fertilizing is not necessary. If the foliage starts to lose its green color, it likely does need to be fertilized. This is more likely if the bulb is large and the pot is a bit small for it. If you have fertilized and the plant does not seem to be regaining its color, re-pot the plant in a larger container.

Be careful not to over-water lily plants, as both the bulb and the roots are susceptible to rot. The plant should be watched for brown foliage, a sign of over-watering. If indoor plant foliage turns brown and the flowers are still intact, the problem is most likely too much water. You can water less often by mulching the top of the soil with about 1 to 2 inches of bark or straw mulch, but you should avoid pine straw.

Aphids can be a problem for lilies. You can rid your plant of aphids in a number of ways, including adding ladybugs to the plant, rubbing away the bugs with a wet wipe, or spraying it with an insecticide. If you are treating your lily for aphids, keep it apart from any other plants until you are sure that every aphid is gone. Aphids can spread quickly from one plant to another.

Like many other bulb plants, you can force your lilies to bloom when you wish. Lilies do not go into a fully dormant state, but they do need a break from sunlight in order to bloom again. To do this, cut back the foliage when it dies and keep the bulb in a cool, dry spot for a few weeks. Then, return the container to the sun, water the soil, and wait for them to sprout and bloom.

Flowers from seeds

Growing flowers from seeds is the least expensive way to grow flowering plants. Flower seeds are extremely inexpensive, and they can be fun to grow. Using a seed flat allows gardeners to grow dozens of different varieties from seed in a small space. These can have as many as 100 small spaces for potting soil and seeds, and the strongest of those are then transplanted into larger containers. Many flowers grow well from seeds, germinating in a few weeks or less and achieving full size in one season.

Marigolds

Botanical name: *Tagetes*

Common name: Marigold

Family name: *Asteraceae*

Origin: North America, South America

Light: Partial shade, full sunlight

Size and growth: 6"-3'

Minimum temperature: 35° Fahrenheit

Blooming season: Summer

Outside hardiness zone: 9-11

Best time to prune: Fall

Pests or diseases to watch for: Slugs

Fertilizer: Granulated flower fertilizer

Unique characteristics/growing tips: Marigolds repel many insects with their scent.

Description:

Marigolds are known for their bright orange and yellow flowers, but there are other varieties available, including red and white, and all of them grow exceptionally well in containers. The flowers will bloom outdoors from about July through the first frost. They grow well indoors, but some people do not care for the fragrance and choose to grow them outdoors because of their strong smell.

Use seed pots or full-size containers of at least 10 inches in width to start the seeds. If you use seed pots, the plant will have to be transplanted after it is a few weeks old. Fill the seed pot or larger container with potting soil and place the seeds on top of the soil. Sprinkle a little potting soil lightly over the seeds, and water the soil until it is moist. Use about three seeds per container, and thin out the seeds after the plants are about three weeks old, leaving only the largest, strongest plant.

Keep the seeds at about 75 degrees and in a spot that gets sunlight each day. If you live in an area that does not get much sun, use a grow light to stimulate germination. UV lights should be placed directly above the seeds in order to stimulate strong growth. Once the marigolds have been thinned and have a few leaves, keep the container in a warm, sunny spot and water them often. Keep the soil slightly moist, but avoid keeping too much water in the pot.

Marigolds have a smell that is offensive to some insects. The plants are sometimes planted alongside plants susceptible to insect infestations in order to keep bugs away. If the soil and watering needs are similar to another plant, the two can be planted in the same container in order to keep insects away from the other. Marigolds are particularly useful to place around vegetable plants to keep damaging bugs away from the crop.

If you have little space for container plants, miniature marigold varieties are available. These can be as small as 10 inches in height, and they grow miniature versions of the well-known pompom shape of marigolds. If you have more space, large versions of the plant grow to as tall as 4 feet in height. Standard plants grow to about 12 to 18 inches in height. If you are planting multiple marigolds in a large planter, plant standard-sized marigolds about 6 inches apart and larger varieties about 18 inches apart.

Whichever variety you choose, it should be kept in full sunlight, though they will tolerate shade in warm climates. The plant will bloom constantly with multiple blooms until the first frost if the sunlight and water requirements are met. For a healthier plant, add a general-purpose, slow-release fertilizer to the soil once each month. Other than watering, marigolds generally need little care. They do not need staking, and most sizes are compact enough to stay in a 10-inch pot without needing transplanting later. Adding mulch will help keep the soil moist, but it is not a requirement. Cutting away the dead flowers, or deadheading, is not needed. If you want your plants to last past the first hard frost, take your outside marigolds indoors when the weather turns cold. Marigolds will not survive a hard freeze.

The only pest that may infest your marigold containers outdoors are slugs. They do not mind the odor of marigolds and can damage stems and leaves. Fortunately, they are large enough to be easily seen and are easy to remove from the plant.

Zinnias

Botanical name: *Zinnia*
Common name: Zinnia
Family name: *Asteraceae*
Origin: North America, South America
Light: Full sunlight
Size and growth: 8"-4'
Minimum temperature: 60° Fahrenheit
Blooming season: Summer, fall
Outside hardiness zone: 3-10
Best time to prune: Fall

Pests or diseases to watch for: Powdery mildew, beetles

Fertilizer: Granulated flower fertilizer

Unique characteristics/growing tips: Zinnias are easy to grow and require little care. Cut away dead flowers.

Description:

Zinnias come in many colors and sizes, and they grow well from seed. The plants are easy to take care of and are well suited for containers. Outdoors, they bloom from summer until the first frost of fall. They bloom on tall stalks and make nice cut flowers as well as nice potted plants for indoor

gardens. The miniature varieties grow to about 1 foot in height, and the largest varieties grow to about 3 feet. Red, pink, white, yellow, white, and flowers with many colors are all possible to grow from seed.

To grow zinnias from seed, plant them on top of potting soil and sprinkle soil lightly over the seeds. Water the soil lightly and wait for them to sprout. They need no other care until they sprout. Once they are a few inches tall, thin out the weaker plants and transfer them into 12-inch containers if you started them in seed flats. If you want to grow many in the same container, space them about 6 inches apart. For the largest varieties, space them about 2 feet apart. Keep the container in full sunlight.

Zinnias are not fussy about their soil, but they will be healthier if some compost is added to the container. Fertilize with a general-purpose, slow-release fertilizer every four weeks. Keep the soil slightly moist at all times. Adding mulch to the soil will help hold moisture. Watering once per day is needed if the plants are outside in hot, sunny conditions. Indoors, watering twice per week is needed. The plant will bloom continuously until the first frost. Cut away dead flowers from the plant to encourage it to produce new blooms and new foliage. Pruning is not needed for the health of the plant, but pruning away any long unproductive foliage can improve the overall look of the plant.

You can help your zinnias to live and bloom longer by bring outdoor containers indoors in the late fall to avoid the frost. Zinnias are generally hardy and resistant to pests and disease, but check the plant periodically for pests such as aphids and mildew. Zinnias can become infected with powdery mildew and blackspot, a plant fungus. Any infected leaves should be cut away. To avoid fungal infections, water at soil level instead of watering the foliage from the top.

Sunflowers

Botanical name: *Helianthus annuus*

Common name: Sunflower

Family name: *Asteraceae*

Origin: North America

Light: Full sunlight

Size and growth: 4-20'

Minimum temperature: 60° Fahrenheit

Blooming season: Summer

Outside hardiness zone: 8-11

Best time to prune: As needed

Pests or diseases to watch for: Sunflower beetles, sunflower moths, grasshoppers, leaf spot disease

Fertilizer: 10-15-10

Unique characteristics/growing tips: Sunflowers track the sun across the sky each day. "Giant" varieties can grow as high as 20 feet.

Description:

A sunflower provides more than just a large and beautiful flower. The seeds are also edible and are popular as a nutritious snack for humans and pets. The largest varieties of sunflowers are so large and eye-catching sunflowers are a hard-to-forget addition to any container garden. For indoor gardens, miniature varieties can accommodate indoor vertical space. Outdoors, you can keep sunflowers that grow to as tall as 20 feet in containers. The largest

 varieties have flowers 2 feet across and produce about 2000 seeds. The miniature varieties produce about 800 seeds. These seeds are actually considered fruits, and they are high in vitamin E, B vitamins, and protein.

Any sunflower that grows to 10 feet or higher is considered a giant variety. Standard sunflower sizes are about 6 to 10 feet in height. Miniature sunflower plants grow to about 4 feet in height and can be as small as 2 feet tall. Giant sunflowers grow one single flower on a tall, thick stalk. Some varieties also grow smaller blooms on the lower branches.

To grow them from seeds in containers, be careful to choose a container large enough for the variety you are growing. Every sunflower should be grown in a pot at least 18 inches in diameter. For giant varieties, a large outdoor planter about 2 feet across is needed. If you are growing your seeds outdoors, place a net or screen over the soil to keep birds from rooting out the seeds. To start them indoors, use seed trays to sprout many seeds at once. The largest of those should be transplanted to the larger containers.

If you want to grow a sunflower plant outdoors, start the seeds indoors a few weeks before the last frost is expected in your area. Start the seeds at or near the surface in peat moss or potting soil, and water the seeds lightly.

Once you have chosen the strongest seedlings, plant giant varieties at least 3 feet apart if you are planting them together in a planter, and plant standard-size sunflowers about 2 feet apart. For miniatures, space the seedlings one foot apart. Make sure the plant has full sunlight for as many hours per day as possible. Sunflowers in partial shade might not live long or be able to produce seeds. Sunflowers are famous for turning their large blooms toward the sun each day and following it across the sky.

The time frame for the plant to grow from seed planting to a mature plant takes about two to three months. The actual number of weeks until maturity will depend on the variety you choose. Water your plant daily, and make sure the container has plenty of drainage. Although drainage is important, do not add sand to the soil. This can make the soil less stable, and the tall stalks need a stable soil in order to withstand the wind.

Fertilize with a 10-15-10 fertilizer when planting, but keep the fertilizer around the edges of the soil instead of near the seeds. Fertilizer can damage seeds, but the growing plant will benefit from the enriched soil. Fertilize the plant again when the flower first starts to bloom.

If you want to harvest the seeds of your sunflower, pull out one seed once the flower begins to die. Open the seed and make certain the inside is full. If so, the seeds are ready to harvest. Cut off the entire flower and hang it somewhere indoors to dry. Hanging it outdoors is a tempting invitation to birds. Allow the flower head and the seeds to dry out. Once dry, you can remove the seeds by hand. Dry seeds will release with gentle pressure.

Outdoor sunflowers can come under attack from birds, squirrels, and ants. Ants will not damage the seeds, but birds and squirrels will eat as many as possible. If they become a problem, consider placing a net over the flower, or place one over just the head to keep birds away.

Sunflowers are hardy plants and will grow well as long as they have plenty of sunshine and water. They generally do not have problems with plant disease. The plants grow as annuals and will die with the first hard freeze though will tolerate a few frosts.

Growing Perennial Flowers in Containers

Perennials are plants that grow back repeatedly for three years or more. These live longer than annuals, which live only one year or one season, and biennials, which live for two years. Growing perennials in containers is one of the easiest ways to keep a container flower garden prospering. With perennials, you do not have to choose more plants for your pots each year or get rid of dead ones to purchase newer plants of the same variety. You can grow the same flowers in the same pots for years, even decades, if you wish. That means less fuss and less time and money spent on keeping beautiful flowers around your home.

Edible Flowers

Edible flowers are an elegant alternative to the standard lettuce and spinach varieties that usually adorn salads. Many of these edibles are well-suited to container gardening. Adding edible flowers to a recipe can change the flavor as well as add an interesting new aesthetic element. Many plants you grow for other reasons, such as for their edible leaves or attractive flowers, also have edible flowers that can be used as edible garnishes or an addition to salads. The following are a few edible flowers that can be grown in containers:

- Marigolds have edible flowers that can be added to rice dishes or salads. The flavor is similar to saffron, and the flowers are sometimes called Poor Man's Saffron. The taste, as well as the bright colors of the flowers, have made them a popular way to dress up pasta dishes as well as soups and herb butters.

- English daisies are edible flowers that might not taste that great (they have a slightly bitter flavor), but they are pretty and edible. They can be used as edible garnishes for any dish.

- Bachelor's buttons, also called cornflowers, are edible and have a sweet flavor with a dash of spiciness. They are often used as a garnish alongside meat, pasta, or vegetable dishes. They have a pretty blue color that can add color to a plate.

- Dandelions are edible and attractive flowers. They are considered weeds and can be extremely invasive, but the leaves and flowers are edible and can be tasty if you pick them while they are young. The older flowers can be a little bitter, but the buds have a sweet taste. They can be used in rice dishes and salads. They are also used to make homemade wine.

- Carnations are edible flowers with a sweet taste. They are often used on cakes as an edible part of the decorations. The base of the flower has a bitter taste, but the petals can be cut away from the base and used in any dish that could use a dash of color.

- Roses are used for so many household uses, including potpourri and in crafts, but they can also be used in everyday cooking. Rose petals have a white lower portion of the petals that has a bitter taste. With that portion removed, rose petals can be used in salads and as a plate garnish for any dish. Because of their beauty and wide variety of colors, they are often used to give a fancy edge to desserts such as ice cream, cake, pastries, and punches. Different varieties of roses have different flavors in their petals, including minty, sweet, and fruity flavors.

- Sunflowers are often grown for their edible seeds, but their petals are also edible. The flowers taste best when they are young, and taste similar to artichokes. They can be used as garnishes, cooked in vegetable dishes, and steamed.

- Peonies are cute flowers that make excellent container flowers, but they also work well in lemonade and other drinks. They go well with desserts and can be sweetened and served alongside tea. They are sometimes used as floating flowers in punches.

- Gladiolus flowers taste similar to lettuce, and they can be used in salads and in sauces. They can also be used in cooked vegetable dishes and as a plate garnish. Before using, remove the anthers, the lobed, end part of the stamen.

- Honeysuckle plants grow wild in many areas, but they are also cultivated in containers for their strong, sweet scent. The taste of honeysuckle flowers is similar to the sweet smell of the flowers, and they can be used in desserts and as cake decorations. Never eat honeysuckle berries, however, as they are highly toxic.

- Impatiens also have a sweet flavor and are used in desserts and tropical drinks.

- Pansies are colorful, compact flowers that have a sweet flavor. Use only the petals to take advantage of the sweetness contained in them, or use the entire flower for a more herbal taste. They can be used in desserts, salads, and fruit dishes.

- Many herb plants have edible flowers in addition to their other uses. Garlic, leeks, and chives are all members of the onion family that produce flowers. Every part of these plants can be eaten, including the flowers. The flavor is dependent on the exact variety you choose and can range from a light onion flavor to a strong garlic taste. They can be used in salads as well as used to flavor soups and vegetables.

- Basil blooms with edible flowers in purple, pink, and white and can be used to flavor fish, rice, and salads. The flavor is a milder version of the flavor of the leaves. There are also varieties that have a minty or lemony flavor that can be used in pasta or fish dishes. They make attractive plate garnishes.

- Borage flowers are edible and attractive with their blue color and star shapes. They have a mild taste similar to cucumbers' and can be used in drinks like lemonade and punch and to garnish tropical drinks. They are also used in soups and dips.

- Chervil has attractive white flowers and a mild flavor similar to anise's. It tends to lose its flavor when it is cooked, but it can be used as a garnish or in salads. Use the fresh flowers instead of drying them in order to keep the flavor.

- Fennel flowers also have a mild flavor similar to anise. The flowers are yellow and star-shaped and can be used in soups, as cake decorations, or as plate garnishes.

- Lavender flowers are prized for their beauty and their scent, but they are also edible. They are often used to garnish desserts like cakes and ice cream. They can be used in sauces, in stews, and as drink garnishes.

- Cilantro flowers can be eaten in salads and with bean and vegetable dishes. Like chervil flowers, they can lose their flavor when cooked. Use raw cilantro flowers for a taste that is much like the leaves of cilantro.

- Jasmine flowers are known all over the world for their beauty and fragrance. However, they are also commonly used to flavor rice and tea. They can give rice and other dishes a distinctive herbal scent prized by many jasmine lovers.

- Rosemary can be used to flavor just about any type of dish, and rosemary flowers can do the same. Mediterranean cooking is particularly well-suited to rosemary flowers. They can be used in everything from meat dishes to desserts. The color of the flowers is dependent on the rosemary variety, but they can be white, blue, pink, or purple. The taste is a milder flavor of the rosemary leaf.

- Mint flowers taste much like the leaves, which makes them an interesting addition to sauces and desserts. With so many varieties of mints available, there are flowers with a wide variety of flavor undertones available.

- Sage flowers come in white, pink, and blue, and they have a mild taste similar to the taste of sage foliage. The flowers are small, at about 1 ½ inches in diameter, and they work well in sauces and bean dishes. They can also be used as a plate garnish alongside fish and chicken dishes.

- Many citrus trees, such as lime, lemon, and orange trees, have edible blooms. Use them sparingly, as their fragrances may interfere with the fragrance of the food you are serving. The taste varies with the fruit type and variety.

- Some vegetable plants also bloom with edible blossoms. Squash flowers are edible, and they have a taste that is similar to a mild squash flavor. The stamens should be removed before eating the flowers. Scarlet runner beans have beautiful red flowers that can be used as a plate garnish and a bright addition to salads and soups.

Succulents

Succulents need little water and very little care, so they make perfect container plants for busy home gardeners. Succulents are plants that come from desert conditions and hang on to every drop of moisture possible, enabling gardeners to water them little and still watch them thrive. With succulents, drainage is extremely important. Too much water will kill a succulent plant quickly. When planting them, add a mixture of about half sand and half potting soil to enable the drainage needed. Water your succulents once a week or less if they are outdoors and about every ten days if they are indoors. Water them less often in the fall, about once every two to three weeks, depending on the variety. During the winter, do not water them at all. They need that period of dormancy in order to grow again in the spring.

Small cactus varieties might need to be re-potted only once every few years or even less often. Many of them are extremely slow growing and will take decades to reach a substantial size. Others might need re-potting every two years as they get larger. If you do need to re-pot your succulents, wait until the plant has flowered and the flowers have died away before attempting the change. This will generally be during the winter.

Outdoor succulent containers are ideal for hot, sunny climates that get little rain. Simply planting the succulents and putting the containers in an area that will allow for their enjoyment is most of their needed care. They can be placed in small tabletop containers, grouped together in large planters to create a rock garden arrangement, or placed in hanging baskets. Indoors, many people choose small succulents because they can be tucked away in tiny spaces among other items and nearly forgotten, and still they will thrive if they have adequate sunlight and not too much water.

Growing succulents is done by many eco-conscious people because they take so little water and require so few resources. If you have outdoor plant watering restrictions, they are perfect for outdoor container gardens in place of plants that would need far more water to thrive.

Some succulents store water in their stems and some store it in their leaves. All will generally have a waxy texture that helps them to keep water inside. All generally need to have full sunlight, including at least six hours of sunlight per day. If your succulents are kept outdoors, protect them from cold temperatures in the winter or bring them inside when frost starts to appear in the mornings.

Do not fertilize succulents often, as they need very few nutrients. If your plant is not growing well, giving it a gentle, slow-release, granulated fertilizer once every spring can be helpful. Never add mulch to the soil. This can trap too much moisture in the soil, which damages the plant's roots. Some people do add gravel or shells to the top of a succulent for aesthetic value, but keep these to a minimum in order to avoid trapping moisture inside the container.

Succulents grow well from cuttings. To grow another plant, simply cut off a leaf or stem and lay it out to dry for a few days. When it is dry, mix up a new succulent potting mixture and place the cutting into it. The cutting will sprout roots and will grow into a new plant. Examples of succulent plants that grow well in containers include aloe, Christmas cactus, and the jade plant.

Common Mistakes to Avoid when Growing Flowers

It is natural to want to grow many flowers together, which adds to the look and smell of a flower garden. However, every plant needs air circulation and room to stretch its roots. Avoid placing plants too closely together because this will damage both plants in the process. To allow flowers plenty of air, avoid placing your containers directly against a house or other structure.

When growing flowers from seeds, avoid placing the seeds too deep into the ground. In nature, flower seeds fall onto the ground and sprout without being covered by more than a light covering of soil. Unless your variety of seeds specify otherwise, give seeds only the barest covering of soil, which allows sunlight to reach the seeds.

Be aware of whether your flowering plant is an annual or a perennial and whether you want to grow the same thing year after year in the same pot. It is easy to see a plant die and assume it is dead, while not realizing it is a perennial that will come back full strength in just a few short months. On the other hand, if you want to choose new flowers each year, choose annuals so that you do not have to bring outdoor perennials indoors for the winter and can simply dump the soil, clean the pot, and plant something brand new.

CASE STUDY: CONTAINER GARDENING TIPS

Anne Marie Choup
The University of Alabama
in Huntsville, associate professor
annemarie.choup@uah.edu

I have grown herbs (basil, cilantro, and sage), flowers (impatiens, marigolds, and daffodils), and tomatoes in containers. Containers are easier to weed and to control soil conditions for specific plants.

Using containers, food can be grown in the kitchen where it can be easily picked and prepared to eat, and plants are protected from birds and rabbits.

The main problems with indoor container gardening are ensuring access to sunlit areas and controlling moisture and mold. The best plant to grow in containers is mint because it would sprawl otherwise.

People are more interested in growing their own food now because it allows them to control pesticides in accordance with their own preferences. It can also provide more affordable food. Some advantages of growing your own food are the sense of accomplishment in eating what you have grown and enjoying the freshest and most local food possible.

Gardeners can get rid of pests without using pesticides by hand-picking and by planting additional plants pests avoid.

Chapter 11

MAINTAINING YOUR PLANTS

Even a hardy plant will need some special care along the way. Every container plant should be monitored and checked for pests, fungi, and bound roots. Most container flowers will also have to be re-potted at some point as well because of expanding size. To be sure that you are ready for each plant's container needs, keep a stock of outgrown containers on hand for re-potting other plants. A simple cabinet or shelf can house many pots stacked within each other and supply pots of different sizes when needed.

Sometimes it is difficult to control every factor of a plant's environment, even indoors. A plant might simply dislike the humidity in your home, or the temperature might be a few degrees over the plant's optimal temperature. Over time, there will undoubtedly be plants you simply have better luck maintaining than others. You can choose to grow more of these and expand the varieties you grow until you have a container garden full of plants that always grow well.

Pest Management

Pests are not as much of a problem for indoor plants as outdoor ones, but you can still get them in your indoor containers. One of the most common are aphids. There are many poisonous aphid sprays on the market, and they do work quickly to get rid of the aphids. However, they are poisonous. Using them might negate your reasons for growing your own food.

Ladybug on a stem with aphids

An alternative is to use ladybugs to control the aphid population. Aphids are the primary food of ladybugs, and letting just a few of them loose on your plants can get rid of your problem quickly without poisoning your produce. Do not be afraid to walk into the nearest nursery and ask for a cup of ladybugs; many nurseries do sell them.

If you have tough outdoor plants, blasting the aphids off the plant with a full-blast stream of water sounds harsh, but it works well. Just do not try this with little seedlings or plants with thin stems.

If the plant is small and you do not have access to ladybugs, try simply picking them off or wiping them away with a damp cloth. Although this is a painstaking process, it can be done for a small to mid-sized plant. A seedling attacked by aphids can generally be saved by pulling all of the aphids off by hand. A larger plant that has a small infestation might respond well to the same.

Roly-polies, also called pillbugs, are neat little creatures, but they can eat your outdoor veggies and snack on the lower leaves and new roots of your plants. To keep them away, just remove any dead leaves and remove or reduce the amount or mulch or dead leaves on the surface of the soil. That is the ideal place for these pests to live, and without it, they will likely move on to a more hospitable area.

Ants are formidable predators because of their enormous numbers. Even if you kill a colony of ants, a new queen can come along and set up shop in the old mound. One of the best ways to get rid of ants taking over a container plant is simply to remove the container and place it elsewhere. Be sure to get rid of ants on the plant before moving it, or the ants will actually find their way back to the mound and then lead the ants to the new location.

If the ants are indoors, kill every ant you see. Then, use soap and water to clean the path that the ants took to reach the plants. This will wash away the chemical trail the ants leave behind to lead their friends to your plant. After that, try to block the entrance to the house with a poison gel or by adding weather stripping to doors to keep bugs out.

Snails and slugs can be devastating to vegetables grown outdoors. They can find their way into containers kept on the ground and eat their way through the skin of your vegetables. They can eat everything from watermelons to squash. They will also eat through the leaves of your fruits and vegetables and might even try chewing through the plant stems.

If slugs and snails are attacking your plants, there are a number of ways to discourage them. The easiest of these is to keep your produce from growing directly on the ground. Slugs and snails like to hide under mulch, rotting leaves and other debris until they are ready to come out and bother your plants. Removing those items will keep the snails and slugs around your plants to a minimum. Avoid using salt to discourage them from your plants. This adds too much salt to the soil and can result in sick plants.

If you have long, trailing vegetables in your containers, such as squash and cucumbers, consider tying the runners to a trellis instead of letting them trail across the ground. Put a tarp around the base of the trellis, and you will have fewer snails and slugs. Using a copper barrier, such as a copper circle around the plant or copper foil around the base, is also thought to discourage snails and slugs. The ions in the copper give snails and slugs a jolt much like a shock of electricity, disrupting their nervous systems.

Beetles are the sworn enemy of many gardeners. They can do an enormous amount of damage to leaves, fruit, and stems. They tend to cluster in enormous numbers and can take over a plant within days. Getting rid of beetles is sometimes attempted with the use of spray pesticides, but these are usually ineffective. The larva of the beetles usually live in the ground, and the spray will not penetrate the soil. The beetles on the plant are likely burrowed within the flowers and will not be affected by the spray. To kill them, they must be hit directly with the spray.

Poison sprays also leave a nasty residue behind that can be unhealthy to humans. If the container is outdoors, it can poison the honeybees that pollinate your plants.

Getting rid of beetles largely comes down to simply pulling them off the plant and discouraging new beetles from joining the party. Carry a bucket of water with a few drops of detergent in it when you de-beetle the plants. When you pick beetles off the plants or shake them out of the flowers, drop them into the bucket to keep them from escaping and coming back again. If a stem or flower seems too overrun with beetles to save, consider simply cutting it off and putting the whole thing into the bucket to be rid of all of the beetles on board.

To deter more beetles from making your plant their home, leave a large, white bucket of water with a small amount of detergent in it on the ground or balcony next to the container. Beetles attracted by the buckets will fly inside to investigate and subsequently drown. The detergent changes the surface tension of the water, which tricks beetles into believing they will be able to pull themselves back out again.

Vegetable plants, fruit trees, berry bushes, and ornamental plants can all be affected by spider mites. These mites are tiny pests, about 1/20 inch in length. They like clustering on the undersides of leaves and can be seen as small dots moving around under a leaf or along a stem. What you might notice before you spot the dots, however, are the webs. As a member of the spider family, they spin tough webs that are easy to spot.

Yellow leaves or leaves with a slight stippling of a light color might be another indication of spider mites. Sometimes this damage is left behind by spider mite colonies that have moved on to another plant. If you see these color problems on a plant's leaves, take a close look at the underside of the leaves before diagnosing the problem as spider mites.

Look closely at any web on your plants to see if there are moving dots inside it. If so, you need to get rid of the mites as soon as possible before they spread. Damage from spider mites can mean dead leaves, which can result in fewer fruit, vegetables, berries, or flowers produced by the plant. On melon and squash plants, the damage from these mites can mean a severely affected crop and even wider-spread damage to the plant. Beans and peas are attacked directly, with mites attacking the pods and leaving the beans and peas injured. Mites are also a particular problem for eggplants and roses grown outside.

Plants that are not getting enough water are especially susceptible to spider mites. Droughts are favorable conditions for spider mites, and the stress that drought puts on plants makes it harder for them to defend themselves. To help prevent the mites from attacking, always keep plants watered regularly to prevent stress on the plant. Oddly, spraying plants for other insects can lead to an invasion of spider mites. When other insects are killed, it gets rid of the many natural predators spider mites have. Avoid general pesticides that kill many types of insects in order to steer clear of spider mites.

Cutting away the affected region is an effective way to get rid of spider mites after they have created a colony on your plant but only if you inspect the rest of the plant to make sure you have not missed any. Leaving a few behind can lead to a brand new colony.

Like aphids, spider mites can be blasted away with a strong stream of water. They can also be killed with insecticidal oil. This is a low-toxicity oil that is particularly effective against mites, and it does not harm wildlife that comes into contact with it. The oils smother the mites instead of using toxicity to poison them. However, these oils do have some level of toxicity, and you should consider the pros and cons before using them on plants you intend to eat.

Grasshoppers are bugs that have historically been one of the worst enemies of cultivated plants. Grasshoppers love to eat anything green, but they will not turn down a meal of carrots, corn, bean, flowers, and onions. If you grow it, there is a good chance they will eat it.

Unlike some of the smaller bugs, it does not take swarms of grasshoppers to cause a lot of damage, though swarms are possible in the early summer. Grasshoppers consume large quantities of fruit, vegetables, and leaves and have been known to cut away large chunks of a plant in little time. An entire plant can be eaten by a few grasshoppers with nothing better to do.

Huge swarms arrive in cycles of every eight to ten years. If you are caught during one of those unlucky years, be grateful your plants are in

containers. You can simply move them inside to avoid the worst of the damage. Before bringing a plant indoors, inspect it thoroughly, especially the inner stems near the bottom of the plant and the undersides of flowers. Having a couple of stowaway grasshoppers will negate the safety of your home, so make sure they do not get a free ride.

The diversion technique works for some gardeners. If you cannot move all of your containers indoors, planting some tall, tempting green grasses around your plants can attract the grasshoppers to them instead of to your plants.

Cutworms are a type of caterpillar that can attack most fruits and vegetables grown outdoors. They particularly love to eat lettuce and often bore into the head to eat the leaves inside. They go after the stems of fruit plants and love to eat seedlings. One of these brown caterpillars can snap off a new seedling. If you have a particularly bad case of cutworms, go out during the night when the cutworms are active and pick them off your produce.

To discourage cutworms from eating your produce in the first place, keep the area around the containers free of weeds. You can also put your containers higher up to keep caterpillars from climbing from other plants onto your container plant. Putting the container on a chair or concrete block will add a barrier between the caterpillars and your plant. If you cannot move the container upward, cover the seedlings with a cloth at night to keep the caterpillars away.

Troubleshooting Common Problems

There are a number of plant diseases and other problems that can wreak havoc in a container garden if the problem is not taken care of. Fortunately, many of these problems can be prevented and treated easily when they occur.

Fungal growth and mildew are some of the most common plant diseases, and they are usually caused by too much moisture within the plant.

Powdery mildew ph phlox

This might be the moisture in the soil, the moisture on the leaves, or even a humidity level far too high for the plant.

If you see fluffy, whitish fuzz on the underside of leaves, you have downy mildew. This fungal disease is aided by cool temperatures and a lot of moisture. Powdery mildew is another form of plant mildew that looks like someone sprinkled white powder onto your plant.

Both mildew issues can be treated by cutting away the infected leaves and stems when possible. Some mildew sprays are effective, but they might not do much for the health of the leaves already affected. Sulphur can be sprayed on the plants to kill the mildew quickly.

To prevent the mildew from returning, conditions of the soil and air need to be remedied. The airflow around the plant should be increased if possible. Move the container away from other plants to increase the air circulation. If the plant is in a container with other plants, take the plant out or prune back the other plants to allow more air circulation for all the plants.

Plants that have leaves that touch the ground are highly susceptible to developing mildew from being exposed to the soil moisture for a long period. If the plant requires moist soil, keep the bottommost leaves pruned to prevent mildew. Inspect the plant regularly to make sure no more white patches are developing on the leaves or stem.

If you are growing onions or chives, watch out for onion white rot. This disease causes the leaves to turn yellow and the bulb to stop growing. Under the soil, the outer skin of the bulb becomes covered with white mold. If this happens, get rid of the plant and the potting soil immediately. Seal the plant in a plastic bag and throw it away. Wash down the container thoroughly to avoid contaminating other plants. To avoid the disease in new onions and chives, give each plant plenty of space. Overcrowding can encourage the growth of this mold. There is no chemical treatment for onion white rot.

Premature fruit drop is a common problem among fruit trees. If you are growing a fruit tree in a container, make sure it is watered and fertilized on a regular schedule. Erratic fruit tree care can cause your fruit to fall before it is ripe, which leaves less ripe fruit for you and your family.

Tomato plants that develop yellow leaves that fall off might be suffering from a magnesium deficiency. Using a fertilizer that has a high potash percentage likely caused the problem. This can be treated by adding Epsom salt to the soil. To add this magnesium remedy, mix about a teaspoon of Epsom salt with a gallon of water and add it to the soil at ground level.

Pruning

How and when to prune any plant is dependent on the plant type and variety. Many plants need to be pruned at the end of their growing season in order to help them go dormant during the late fall and winter. Others need little or no pruning at all to help them complete their yearly cycle.

Deadheading, cutting away dead flowers, is a common pruning technique that essentially fools plants into producing more flowers. By cutting away the flowers before they have fully dried, the flower does not get the chance to let seeds fall into the soil. The only choice for self propagation is to produce more flowers.

Virtually every plant will benefit from having its dead leaves and stems cut away. Dead foliage is unhealthy for a plant, as it interferes with sunlight and air circulation but does not add to the plant's energy. It might also harbor insects that feast on rotting foliage. Dead leaves and stems are also aesthetically unpleasing to plant owners.

Fruit plants generally benefit from being pruned during their winter dormancy. However, many other plants, such as roses, will push themselves to produce new growth when old growth is cut away, and those generally need spring pruning if the containers are kept outdoors. The new growth should occur in the spring and summer to allow it to be mature enough to make it through the following winter's cold weather.

Although pruning some plants, such as grape plants, can be complicated, the wrong pruning methods generally will not lead to the death of a plant. It might lead to less fruit or a plant that has too much foliage or an overly long shape, but it will generally not affect the plant's overall health. When you prune a plant, always make sharp cuts with clippers or a hand pruner. Twisting the plant or ripping away branches can leave it vulnerable to pests and disease.

In general, flowering shrubs and trees need to be pruned after their flowers have died, but there are some exceptions. Be sure you know exactly when your particular plant should be pruned before you tackle any major pruning tasks other than clearing away dead growth.

Replanting

If you see roots growing around the outside of the soil in a circular growth pattern, your plant is root bound, which is a result of being in a pot much too small for the plant's size. When a plant is root bound, it will have trouble getting the nutrients it needs through the roots. It might even have trouble loosening its roots enough to adapt to a larger pot.

To help a root-bound plant, break up the outer root growth. Those roots are not able to take in nutrients in their current position, so damaging them will not adversely affect the plant. You can break up the outer, circular roots with your hands by simply pulling the roots outward, or you can use scissors or a trowel to do it.

Most plants you buy in a nursery or a grocery store will need to be re-potted quickly. It is rare to purchase a plant, seedling, or mature, from a nursery or grocery store that is not at least a little root bound. Plan to re-pot anything you buy, and save the original pot to plant something smaller.

For plants already growing in containers, it can be hard to tell exactly when the plant needs re-potting without inspecting the roots. Occasionally, you should pull the plant out of its container slightly to inspect the roots. If you see the beginnings of the circular growth, it is time to re-pot the plant.

An easy sign of bound roots is growth that slows or stops all together. This happens in young plants when the roots can no longer bring in nutrients from the soil because the root density is too high.

Learning From Others

Learning more about gardening from other gardeners can help you to learn to maintain your plants in your own climate. Often, there are things to learn about your own region, such as severe weather precautions, special shortcuts that can be taken, and plants that grow well in your climate that other people in your area can teach you. Learning about gardening from others is usually easy because of the many gardening groups related to certain types of gardening and specific types of plants. Often, help can be found for free.

Taking gardening classes

Taking gardening classes can help you learn to take care of one specific type of plant or one category of plants, such as annuals. It can also simply give you some basic plant care tips and experience. Home improvement stores often hold weekend gardening classes that concentrate on specific plant categories. These classes are often free in order to encourage new customers to visit the store.

For busy gardeners and those in remote areas, there are online gardening classes. These can be online auditing of a university's gardening courses, or they can be free courses. Some are offered to help people save water when gardening or to integrate local plant life into their gardening to save resources. Local gardening classes often teach students when to water plants and what types of plants are best suited for the local climate.

Swapping seeds and seedlings

Local gardening groups often host seed swaps for members and the community as a whole. Additionally, public gardens sometimes arrange seed swaps done during meetings or maintenance volunteer sessions. There might also be a public seed-swapping box open for any community member to take and/or leave seeds.

If your local area does not have a seed-swapping group already, consider starting your own. Home gardening is such a popular hobby there are likely people in your own community who would be happy to have new seeds to try and to save some of their favorite ones to give away.

Finding local help

The Cooperative Extension System is a national network of educational services funded by the government that offers a wide range of gardening assistance. An extension office is located in every state with satellite offices scattered throughout the state. These offices are open to gardeners who want some advice or assistance with their gardening. This can include helping you to decide what to grow based on the local climate and the nutritional needs of your family as well as more specific help with your soil and your indoor or outdoor plants.

Each extension office has professionals in various horticultural fields who are qualified to help with soil problems, wildlife problems, and more. They can recommend when to plant specific plants in your climate and what local pests might become a problem. If you have a plant infected with a disease spreading among your plants, the extension office can give you advice for eradicating it.

Some extension offices offer gardening classes for various levels of gardening expertise. The extension office also gives the master gardener title to those who complete all of the required training and the number of service hours required. Master gardeners are available at some extension offices to answer gardening questions or even to assist in re-potting and other tasks. Extension officials can help identify a pest from your garden or a specific plant species you find growing there. Most assistance offered by the Cooperative Extension System is free, though some services will cost a small fee. Find your local extension office through the USDA's site at **www.csrees. usda.gov/Extension**.

Conclusion

With a small investment in supplies and containers, a home gardener can grow flowers, fruits, vegetables, and herbs with a little dedication to observance and care. Container gardening can save you money on groceries and fresh flowers and add beauty to your home for as long as you want to care for your plants.

Anyone Can Garden in Containers

You do not have to have a lot of experience in gardening to grow plants in containers. Growing up on a farm or being a *Little House on the Prairie* enthusiast is not required to be able to grow your own fruit, vegetables, herbs, and flowers at home. It is possible, with a little care, the right tools, and some basic knowledge of plant growth, to grow a nice container garden inside or outside of your home.

Any age group can get involved with growing plants in containers, from preschoolers to the elderly. It is rewarding for anyone of any age to see what their efforts can produce.

Container Gardening is Flexible, Affordable, and Fun

Container gardening mixes all of the great things about home gardening with the wonderful things about outdoor gardening. With container gardening, you are still able to get your hands dirty by sifting through soil and touching the roots of plants. You get back to the earth and watch life start and grow.

However, unlike when you grow your plants directly in the ground, you get the flexibility of a portable garden. Your container garden can be moved around, changed, taken with you to a new home, or sent to stay with a friend while you are on vacation. It can be as large or as small as you want it to be, no matter how much ground space you do or do not have. It is not dependant on the weather or factors beyond your control.

Container gardening indoors is also easier physically than gardening outdoors, and it can be done no matter what the weather. It can be done at any time of the year and at any time of day or night.

To get started, think about what you want to grow and why you want to grow it. You might choose to plant a few ornamental flowers and a few fruits and vegetables to begin. As you start growing plants in containers, you will find favorites you want to grow year after year, but continue to experiment with new ones to find new favorites. This will keep your container garden ever changing and new even as you grow plants you have come to love over the years.

USDA PLANT HARDINESS ZONE MAP

The USDA Plant Hardiness Zone Map divides the United States into specific temperature zones. Each zone has a temperature range to make it easier to determine which plants can be grown in that zone. Most seedlings and seed packets come with a zone range that allows gardeners to understand exactly where they can be safely planted. Each zone has its own color and a number between one and 11.

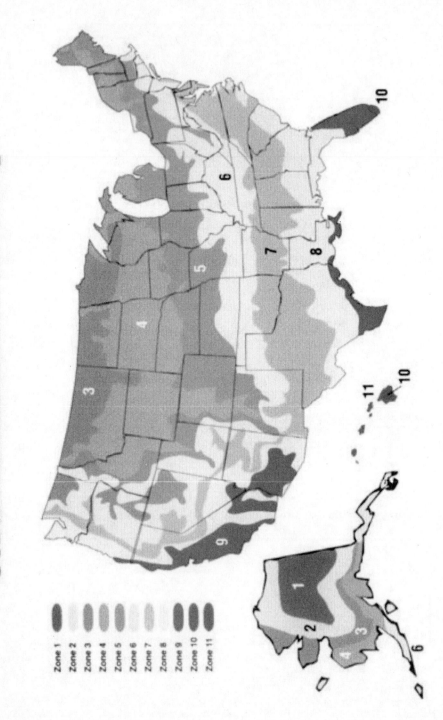

USDA Plant Hardiness Zone Map

Bibliography

BBC, "Grow Onions and Garlic,"
www.bbc.co.uk/gardening/basics/techniques/growfruitandveg_ growingonions1.shtml.

Berry, Susan, *Kitchen Harvest*, London: Frances Lincoln, 2002.

Bewaterwise.com, "California Friendly Landscape and Gardening Classes," **www.bewaterwise.com/training01.html**.

Buckingham, Alan and Jo Whittingham, *Grow Vegetables*, New York: DK Publishing, 2008.

Brooklyn Botanical Garden, "Introduction: The Potted Garden," **www.bbg.org/gardening/handbook/the_potted_garden/#/tabs-2**, 2010.

Floridata, "Coriandrum sativum," **www.floridata.com/ref/c/cori_sat.cfm**, 2010.

GardenWeb, "Zip Code to USDA Zone Finder," **www.gardenweb.com/zones/zip.cgi**, 2006.

Gerlach, Linette, "How To Grow Grapes: Choosing Varieties, Vines, Pruning, Trellis," How to Do Things, **www.howtodothings.com/home-and-garden/a4255-how-to-grow-grapes.html**.

Growing Beans, "Beans: How to Grow Them and More," **http://growingbeans.org**, 2009.

Healthy Child Healthy World, "10 Fruits and Vegetables to Buy Organic," **http://healthychild.org/live-healthy/checklist/10_fruits_and_vegetables_to_buy_organic**.

Herb Expert, "Common Problems When Growing Herbs," **www.herbexpert.co.uk/CommonProblemsWhenGrowingHerbs.html**, 2010.

Hom, Louis, "About Organic Produce," University of California at Berkeley, **www.ocf.berkeley.edu/~lhom/organictext.html**, 1996-2009.

Home Improvement Pages, "Growing Succulents," **www.homeimprovementpages.com.au/article/Growing_Succulents**.

Iannotti, Marie, "Borage – Growing and Using the Herb Borage" About.com, **http://gardening.about.com/od/herbsspecificplants1/p/Borage.htm**, 2010.

Jackson, Deb and Karen Bergeron, "Angelica Herb," Alternative Nature Online Herbal, **www.altnature.com/gallery/angelica.htm**, 2007.

Jauron, Richard, "Growing Currants and Gooseberries in the Home Garden," Iowa State University Extension, **www.ipm.iastate.edu/ipm/hortnews/1995/3-17-1995/curr.html**.

Joys of Lavender, "Growing Lavender," **www.joys-of-lavender.com/growing-lavender.html**, 2009.

McGee, Rose Marie Nichols and Maggie Stuckey, *The Bountiful Container*, New York: Workman Publishing, 2002.

National Center for Complementary and Alternative Medicine, "St. John's Wort and Depression," **http://nccam.nih.gov/health/stjohnswort/sjw-and-depression.htm**, 2007.

Odum, Sally, "A Medicinal Herb Garden," Suite 101, **http://vegetablegardens.suite101.com/article.cfm/a_medicinal_herb_garden**, 2007.

Pizzorno, Jr., Joe, "Integrative Medicine and Wellness," WebMD, **http://blogs.webmd.com/integrative-medicine-wellness/2007/08/fresh-frozen-or-canned.html**, 2007.

Salman, David, "Sage Advice," Fine Gardening, **www.finegardening.com/design/articles/salvias-sage-perennial.aspx**.

Schalau, Jeff, "How Seeds Work," Backyard Gardener, **http://ag.arizona.edu/yavapai/anr/hort/byg/archive/howseedswork.html**, 2007.

The Gardener's Network, "How to Grow Zucchini Squash," **www.gardenersnet.com/vegetable/zucchini.htm**.

The United States National Arboretum, "USDA Plant Hardiness Zone Map," **www.usna.usda.gov/Hardzone/ushzmap.html**, 2004.

University of Florida IFAS Extension, "Blueberry Gardener's Guide," **http://edis.ifas.ufl.edu/mg359**.

University of Nebraska-Lincoln Nematology, "What are Nematodes?" **http://nematode.unl.edu/wormgen.htm**.

Author Biography

Lizz Shepherd received a Bachelor of Arts in journalism from Auburn University and has been growing container plants since junior high school. She runs Waxing Moon Marketing from home and grows vegetables, herbs, and flowers from container and in-ground gardens.

Index

A

Amaryllis, 235-237, 239

Ant, 263

Aphid, 203, 244, 262

B

Basil, 78, 105-106, 134-135, 137, 140, 182, 222, 243, 255, 260

Bean, 76-77, 153, 157-158, 170, 256, 266

Beetle, 162, 174, 180

Blackberry, 71, 77, 192-193

Blueberry, 281, 75, 185, 189-191

Borage, 280, 106-108, 255

Bulb, 71, 111, 117, 135, 164-165, 168-169, 231-244, 268

C

Cantaloupe, 206-207

Carrot, 139, 145, 159-161

Caterpillar, 267

Chamomile, 41, 102, 108-109, 134, 137, 140

Chives, 40-41, 110-111, 135, 143, 255, 268

Christmas cactus, 46, 259

Cilantro, 112-114, 116, 134, 256, 260

Clay, 20, 57-58, 60, 81

Climate, 19, 21, 35-37, 45, 52, 122, 165-166, 169, 171, 181-182, 190, 193, 195, 199, 201, 214-215, 219, 234, 238, 271-272

Clippers, 73, 270

Companion planting, 98-99

Concrete, 58-59, 61, 97, 181, 267

Cooperative Extension System, 272-273

Cucumber, 30, 70, 77, 86, 109, 145, 154, 161-163, 179-180

Cultivating fork, 75

Currant, 200-203

D

Daffodil, 232-233

Dappled light, 23-24, 99

Deadheading, 131, 247, 269

Dill, 113-116, 134, 143

Drainage, 28, 52-53, 60, 64-67, 81-82, 86, 103, 106, 116, 118, 125, 130, 132, 141-142, 147-148, 159-160, 167, 169, 173, 175, 179, 181, 186, 190, 192-193, 196, 204, 212, 214, 229, 233-234, 241, 251, 257

E

Evening primrose, 41

F

Fennel, 115-117, 123, 134-135, 140, 255

Fertilizer, 20, 23, 31, 62, 71-72, 82, 84-85, 98, 105-110, 112-115, 117-118, 120-126, 129-130, 132, 141-142, 156-157, 159, 161, 163, 166-170, 172, 175-176, 178-180, 189, 191-200, 202-204, 206-213, 215-216, 218, 220, 225, 227-229, 231-233, 235-238, 240, 243-245, 247-249, 251, 258, 269

Fungal growth, 156, 169, 173, 175, 218, 267

Fungi, 83, 86, 96, 148, 156-157, 159, 161, 169, 171-173, 175, 178, 197, 212, 215-216, 219, 229, 261

G

Garden pot, 136

Garlic, 279, 163-165, 255

Germination, 90, 93, 109, 111, 127, 152-153, 164-165, 246

Gladiolus, 230, 240-242, 254

Glass, 60-61, 73, 127

Glove, 70-71

Gooseberry, 194-195

Grape, 203-206, 217, 219, 270

Grow light, 246

H

Hanging pot, 62

Hardiness zone, 277, 281, 36, 105-108, 110, 112-113, 115, 117, 120-122, 124, 126, 129, 132, 156, 159, 161, 163, 165-166, 168, 170, 172, 174, 176, 179, 189, 191-192, 194-198, 200, 203, 206, 208-209, 211, 213, 216, 227, 232-233, 235, 238, 240, 242-243, 245, 247, 249, 18

Heat lamps, 45

Heirloom, 39, 91-92, 149, 183, 222

Herb garden, 281, 22, 52, 91, 133-134, 136

Honeydew, 209-210

Humidifier, 50

Hyacinth, 158, 231, 237-240

Hybrid, 92-93, 197, 228, 230

Hypocotyl, 93

I

Insecticidal oil, 130, 266

L

Ladybug, 262

Lavender, 280, 46, 102-103, 117-119, 133, 140, 256

Lemon, 42, 50, 101-102, 119, 134, 136, 185, 188, 196-199, 217, 220, 257

Lettuce, 33, 40, 48, 88, 146, 148, 151, 155-156, 165-167, 252, 254, 267

Lily, 24, 67, 240, 242-244

Lime, 42, 50, 185, 188, 198-200, 220, 257, 12

M

Magnesium deficiency, 269

Marigold, 98, 245-247

Mildew, 59-60, 114-115, 126, 128-129, 141, 148, 155, 176, 179-181, 189, 191, 193-195, 204, 206-210, 213, 215, 219, 227, 230, 248-249, 267-268

Mint, 24, 49, 101-103, 118-121, 134, 137, 140, 222, 256, 260

N

Nitrogen, 85, 106, 112, 157, 234

O

Onion, 110, 164, 168-169, 255, 268

Onion white rot, 268

Orange, 39, 41, 185, 195-197, 199, 217, 228, 232, 236, 238, 245, 257

Oregano, 121-123, 134-135, 139-140

Organic, 280, 22-23, 30-31, 39, 53, 81-85, 88, 109, 111-113, 120-121, 125, 129-130, 132, 140-142, 147, 152, 154, 160, 163-164, 173, 175, 179-180, 183, 187, 190, 220, 223, 233-234, 239-241

Oversized planter, 63-64

Oxygen, 93, 95

P

Paper, 59-60, 153, 208

Parsley, 113, 123-126, 133-135, 146

Pea, 170-172

Peach, 185-186, 211-212, 228, 232

pH, 84, 147, 189-190, 201, 210, 219, 234, 267

Phosphorus, 85, 107

Plastic, 27, 57-58, 60, 74, 76, 94, 97, 173, 181, 186, 210, 268

Potassium, 85, 200

Potato, 135, 172-174

Prune, 71, 73, 105, 107-108, 110, 112-113, 115, 117-118, 120, 122, 124, 126, 128-129, 132-133, 139, 156, 159, 161, 163, 166, 168, 170, 172, 174, 176, 179, 189, 191-195, 197-198, 200, 203, 205-206, 208-209, 211, 213, 216, 227, 230, 232-233, 235, 238, 240, 243, 245, 247, 249, 268-270

Pruning shears, 73

R

Radicle, 93

Raspberry, 191-192

Recycled, 27, 59, 61, 66, 79, 8-9

Root bind, 96

Root system, 41, 65

Rose, 281, 71, 227-230, 253

Rosemary, 44, 49, 78, 101-102, 126-129, 134-135, 139-140, 182, 256, 17, 11

S

Sage, 281, 46, 101, 129-131, 134-135, 139-140, 256, 260

Seed-swapping, 272

Shovel, 71-72

Slug, 125, 216

Spider mite, 203, 265

Spinach, 146, 151-152, 155-156, 166, 174-176, 252

Squash, 41, 62-63, 70, 77, 145-146, 149, 154-155, 161, 176-179, 181, 206, 208-209, 257, 263, 265, 281

St. John's wort, 40-41, 102, 137-138, 281

Stake, 76-77, 162-163, 165, 171, 212, 241-242

Strawberry, 47, 63, 68, 86, 213-216, 218-219

Succulents, 280, 41, 78-79, 257-258

Sulphur, 189-190, 268

Sunflower, 249-251

T

Thyme, 44, 131-135, 137, 139

Tomato, 33, 64, 70, 76-77, 79-80, 86, 92, 143, 183, 216-218, 222, 269

Tomato cage, 77

Transplanting, 56, 71, 94-95, 98, 104, 113, 116, 204, 209, 247

Trellis, 280, 47, 62, 76-77, 145-146, 161-163, 171, 193, 203, 205-206, 210, 217, 220, 263

Trowel, 71-72, 75, 95, 270

Tulip, 233-235

U

United States Department of Agriculture, 18

USDA, 277, 279, 281, 36-37, 273

W

Watering can, 25, 67, 73-74, 86, 149

Watering granules, 86

Watermelon, 77, 207-209

White pine blister rust, 200-201

Window box, 62-63, 231

Wood, 59, 97, 191, 202, 241

Z

Zinnia, 247

Zucchini, 281, 145, 177-181